CHRISTIANS IN PERSIA

1. The above two couplets are taken from the third book of the Mathnaví of Jalálu'ddín Rúmí, the greatest of the Persian mystical poets. The reference is clearly to the raising by our Lord of the widow's son at Nain, as recorded in St Luke's Gospel, vii, 11–16. The illustration is by Musavvir ul Mulk, the famous miniature painter of Isfahan. The words may be rendered into English as follows:

Oh! do not deem the words of Christ mere sound and breath,
But note there fled away from Him the spectre of Death!
Deem not his accent rough, His style inerudite,
See how the dead man leapt to life, and sat upright!

CHRISTIANS IN PERSIA

ASSYRIANS, ARMENIANS
ROMAN CATHOLICS AND PROTESTANTS

BY

ROBIN E. WATERFIELD

London
GEORGE ALLEN & UNWIN LTD
RUSKIN HOUSE   MUSEUM STREET

First published in 1973

© George Allen & Unwin Ltd 1973

ISBN 0 04 275001 6 hardback
     0 04 275002 4 paper

Printed in Great Britain
in 11 point Baskerville type
by Clarke, Doble & Brendon Ltd
Plymouth

Preface

This book was substantially researched and written during the six months, January to June 1971, and owes a very great deal to a number of friends and libraries who have rendered me the greatest assistance. I am especially indebted to the USCL and the SPCK for financial assistance during the preparation of the book. The Reverend Dick and Mrs Ashton gave me lodging and much other help besides, Mr John Gurney of Oxford read the typescript and made many pertinent comments and corrections, Mr John Hananian of Tehran provided a mass of stimulating comment and criticism, Michael Harverson gave continuous encouragement and help in all stages of the book's production, and finally my old friend and master, Canon M. A. C. Warren, was warmly encouraging and helpful as always.

I am also indebted to the following persons for information and assistance of many kinds: Father William Barden O.P., the Reverend H. E. J. Biggs, Mme Bouteloup, Hugh Carless, Miss Vera Eardley, Dr Stella Henriques, Miss Mary Isaac, Dr Jim Laster, Mrs Maddock (grand-daughter of Robert Bruce), the Reverend George Malcolm (son of Napier Malcolm), Dr W. McE Miller, Dr Ronald Pont, Mrs Violette Rake, Dr Paul Seto, the Reverend Norman Sharp, Bishop W. J. and Mrs Thompson and Mr and Mrs Henry Ward. I am also greatly indebted to the staffs of the Fulham Central Library, the London Library, the Catholic Central Library and the British Museum as well as the authorities of the Church Missionary Society and the Church's Ministry among the Jews for much help. There are many others too numerous to name to whom I also owe thanks, which I do most heartily give.

I need hardly add that the mistakes are all my own. I am conscious that the book may not entirely please either scholars or the general public. My hope is that it may have collected in one volume a body of facts and information hitherto only to be found widely scattered in a great number of different places, and that it may encourage others to study some parts of this history in greater depth.

January 1972   *Tehran*

*To the Christians of Persia
past, present and future*

Contents

Illustrations

Part One

THE NESTORIAN PLANTING

Chapter One

THE BACKGROUND

Iran, the land better known to us as Persia, has a recorded history of some 2,500 years, but human settlements have been found dating back to 10,000 BC and a more or less continuous record of settlement can be traced from 5000 BC. Around 1800 BC the first wave of Aryans migrating from Transoxiana reached Iran, and it is from them that Iran received its name. Six hundred years later a second wave of migrants arrived, bringing with them their own religion and the Vedic Pantheon of Gods.

The first group in Iran to form a definite kingdom was the Medes who in alliance with the Scythians and the Babylonians attacked Assyria in 612 BC and destroyed its capital, Nineveh, thus becoming the overlords of the great Assyrian Empire. Just over fifty years later, in fact in 559 BC, Cyrus, heir to a petty dynasty in South Persia, overthrew his Median overlord, Astyages, and established the Achaemenian dynasty. Here, for the Persians, begins the history of their monarchy, which has endured as an institution for over twenty-five centuries and, as the recent celebrations show, is still a potent factor in the life of the country.

The dynasty founded by Cyrus (who fully deserved the title 'Great' which was accorded to him) was unparalleled by any previous one in its extent, its organisation, artistic achievement, and religious tolerance and respect for human rights. Its influence on Persian life and thought throughout the ages has been immense, and is still strongly felt today. This has been clearly demonstrated during the recent 2,500th anniversary celebrations.

One of the distinctive features of the period covered by the Achaemenian dynasty is the long drawn out war with the Greeks, who prevented Persia from expanding to the West. This war was finally settled in the reign of Darius III when the Greeks, under the leadership of the young Alexander of Macedon, attacked Persia. By a series of brilliant military marches, Alexander traversed Asia Minor

11

and in 333 BC met and defeated the armies of Darius near the Cilician Gates at Issus. Alexander did not wait to consolidate his victory but pressed on eastwards. In 331, after capturing Tyre and making a detour into Egypt, he crossed the Euphrates and moved towards the village of Gaugamela near Arbela, where Darius had made his camp. On 1 October 331 the battle was fought which sealed the fate of the Persian Empire. Alexander next pushed on into the heartland of Persia, the province of Fars, and reached Persepolis, the site of Darius' sacred palace and the symbolic heart of the Persian Empire, where he stayed until the spring of 330. During his stay there the palace was burnt, whether on purpose or by accident we shall probably never know. But whether the fire was accidental or intended, the destruction of Persepolis was a devastating psychological blow to Persian pride, and was seen by all as revenge for the burning of the Acropolis and the Great Temple at Babylon.

Until now Alexander had simply been the general acting on behalf of the League of Corinth in the prosecution of a war against the Persians. This assignment was now completed; henceforward Alexander acted on his own initiative – driven forward by his own ambitions and ideals. Alexander had been a pupil of Aristotle and had been greatly influenced by him and by Aristotle's older contemporary, Isocrates. These philosophers had propounded the concept of *homonoia*, a word which can roughly be translated as 'a being of one mind together'. Aristotle had propounded this idea as being the means whereby the various Greek city states might settle their differences, but he had never thought of applying it to anyone but the Greeks. But according to Eratosthenes, Alexander 'believed that he had a mission from God to harmonise men generally and to be the reconciler of the world, bringing men from everywhere into a unity and mixing their lives and customs, their marriages and social ways, as in a loving cup'. A modern writer has summed up Alexander's achievement in this way :

Alexander united the whole civilised world for the first time under a single head and gave to it a common language and culture. By the natural gifts of his extraordinary personality, he at the same time set before it a perfect model of kingship and thus ensured the persistence of the monarchical principle for two millennia. This, his conscious work, had a direct effect on the evolution of monotheism, while in other respects his conquests proved the turning point in the history of religions. . . . Before his coming we see the ancient world divided into separate communities each with its own pantheon and forms of worship . . . but immediately after, all this is changed. The interchange of ideas between East and West has thrown the religions of the world into the melting-pot in which the germs of a different grouping of the human race are dimly visible (Legge, *Forerunners and Rivals of Christianity* (1915), Vol. 1, pp. 26–7).

It was this vision of a world state living in peace and harmony that inspired Alexander and enabled him to reconcile those who were turning against him. At the great feast at Opis in 324 BC, when Macedonians and Persians sat down together and poured a libation from the great *Krater* or loving cup, Alexander prayed that they might in future be one commonwealth and live in *homonoia* together. Sir William Tarn was surely not exaggerating when he called Alexander 'the man whose career was one of the dividing lines of world history'. Alexander's ideals have had many echoes since that time: the Mazdakite dream of late Zoroastrianism and the Christian and Muslim ideals of the universal brotherhood of man were all foreshadowed in Alexander's youthful idealism. Perhaps only Christianity has understood fully the price that mankind must pay for the realisation of such a dream. The fact that Alexander, or Iskandar as he is known to the Persians, is the enemy *par excellence* of Persia, has not diminished his stature in their eyes.

On the death of Alexander in 323 BC his Empire was divided between his generals. The main portion, including Persia, was inherited by Seleucus. Seleucus may have hoped to continue Alexander's policies (he had married a Persian princess), but he and his successors preferred to live in Syria and paid little attention to the eastern parts of their kingdom. Less than 100 years later, these revolted and the Arsacid dynasty of Parthia came into being. At its greatest extent the Parthian kingdom extended from Afghanistan to the Tigris and from the Caspian Sea to the Persian Gulf.

THE RISE OF ZOROASTRIANISM

Most of Alexander's ideals seemed irrevocably lost, but through the intermarriage which he encouraged and the cities which he founded, Greek culture and art spread throughout Persia and Central Asia.

13

The Parthian kingdom lasted until AD 270, during which time the Romans replaced the Greeks as the enemy in the West. But Hellenistic culture was remarkably longlived, as may be gathered from the fact that centuries after Alexander's death when the Parthians overcame the Consul Crassus, the Roman prisoners were surprised to find their Armenian Arsacid captors enjoying the plays of Euripides. Nevertheless, the Parthians were Persians at heart, as Ghirshmann writes: 'By their revival of the Iranian spirit and their successful foreign policy, the Parthian-Arsacids prepared the way for the Sassanians, who were enabled to achieve a national unity and a civilisation that was more exclusively Iranian than it had ever been before (Ghirshmann, *Iran*, p. 288).

The Seleucid period had been a time of foreign domination and of cultural and religious ferment. The Parthian era had seen the absorption of foreign influences and the gradual rise of a national consciousness, not least in the matter of religion. The dominant religion of the Achaemenian period had, by the reign of Artaxerxes I (*c.* 441 BC), become Zoroastrianism. By the time of the Parthians, therefore, Zoroastrianism had already had a long and chequered career. Its founder, Zoroaster (? 628–551 BC), was probably a Median by birth, who attempted to reform the prevailing religion of his time, inherited from the Aryans and about which we know very little. He was opposed by the priestly caste and was forced to migrate eastwards to the kingdom of Chorasmia (now north-east Persia and western Afghanistan), where he was supported by the King, Vishtaspa.

In its original form the religion of Zoroaster was monotheistic and only dualistic in its ethics. Gradually this new religion moved westwards and for a time was as popular as the older religions. Religious rites and practices of whatever kind were in the hands of the *Magi* whose position, as Professor Zaehner says, 'would seem to correspond to that of the Levites among the Jews, or, even more closely, to that of the Brahmans in India; they were a hereditary caste entrusted with the supervision of the national religion, whatever form it might take and in whatever part of the Empire it might be practised' (Zaehner, *Dawn and Twilight of Zoroastrianism*, p. 163). Under the influence of the *Magi* many new elements were introduced and the simple monotheism of Zoroaster was lost; a religion far removed from his original teaching was gradually developed, strongly dualistic and with a rigid caste system.

14

With the rise of the Sassanian dynasty in AD 226 there was a revival of Persian nationalism and with this a desire to purify and strengthen the national religion and make it an instrument of state policy. The Sassanians continued the reaction against the religious and cultural pluralism, which had begun under the Parthians. They made the Zoroastrian religion and unrelenting opposition to the West the twin pillars of their national policy.

Various monarchs at various times flirted with unorthodox ideas. Shapur I, for instance, was interested in Manichaeism, and Kavad nearly destroyed his kingdom by his adherence to the Mazdakite heresy. Various members of the Sassanian dynasty gave greater or lesser support to Christianity as the general situation seemed to demand, but fundamentally they disapproved of all religions except Zoroastrianism and of all people except the Persian-speaking Aryans of the high plateau. Unfortunately, Persia has constantly found itself in contact with alien religions and alien races, some of whom have conquered the country or have for long periods been its rulers.

Such, briefly, was the situation and its background when Christians became an organised religious community in Persia round about AD 200.

15

Chapter Two

CHRISTIANITY IN IRAN TO THE END OF THE SASSANIAN DYNASTY

The tradition that the three kings who came to worship Christ at his birth were Persians is so old and honourable that one must begin with it. An earlier historian of Christian missionary work in Iran began his book by quoting from St John Chrysostom's sixth Homily on Matthew's Gospel where he writes:

> The Incarnate Word on coming to the world gave to Persia, in the persons of the *Magi*, the first manifestations of His mercy and light . . . so that the Jews themselves learn from the mouths of Persians of the birth of their Messiah. *Persico sermone didicerunt quae prophetis nuntiantibus discere noluerunt.*

Still within the Gospel narrative we may hazard a guess that news of the new religion was also brought to Iran by some of those Parthians, Medes and Elamites whom Luke mentions as being present in Jerusalem on the Day of Pentecost. Perhaps some of these men and women may have brought to Iran the first rumours of the new religion, or may even have practised it themselves.

A very old tradition represents the Apostle Thomas as having brought Christianity to Parthia as well as to India – though later traditions mention only India. If we remember, however, that the Parthian Empire included present-day Afghanistan and quite a large portion of Northern India, then the two traditions are not irreconcilable. Tertullian and others confirm that there were Christians in Persia before the Sassanians and that by AD 220 the Church had some organisation with a number of loosely federated episcopal sees.

More certain are the links between Christianity in Persia and Christianity in the little state of Osrhoene on her western borders, whose capital city, Edessa (modern Urfa in Turkey), was an important staging post on the trade route between the East and the

16

Mediterranean. The tradition that the King of Edessa, Abqar, corresponded with Jesus or that the apostles, Thomas and Thaddaeus, or St Simon the Zealot brought the faith to the city must reluctantly be dismissed as baseless. But we know that by about AD 150, while Edessa was still part of the Parthian Empire, Christianity existed there and that by 190, when a controversy arose about the date of Easter, there were numerous bishoprics all over the Parthian Empire and Edessa itself was a flourishing Christian centre. It is possible that about this time the King was baptised since on coins minted between 180 and 192 a cross appears on the headdress of King Abqar VIII.

Edessa, from its origins as a Christian centre, came under the ecclesiastical control of the Patriarch of Antioch. Antioch was a largely Greek-speaking city, whereas, since the eighth century BC, the inhabitants of the Mesopotamian basin had spoken various dialects of the Semitic language Aramaic, not unlike the language spoken in Palestine at the time of Jesus. The eastern Aramaic dialect of Edessa was to become the literary and liturgical language of the Eastern Church there and later of the Church in Persia, where the language was also widely used for official and business purposes. The literary language known as Syriac produced a fine body of Christian literature and is still used by the remnant of the ancient Church in Persia and Iraq to this day.

Osrhoene, being a border state, was continuously involved in the wars between Rome and Parthia and later between Rome and the Persian Empire. In AD 216 the Romans conquered it and occupied it. So from the very earliest times it was torn between East and West and the uncertainty as to which side it was really on was one of the underlying causes of many future disputes. This tension is seen in one of the greatest Christian writers of Edessa, Tatian (born 150), whose only surviving original work is a violent diatribe against the Greeks – their culture, philosophy and religious ideas. His other work, *The Diatessaron* or harmony of the Gospel narratives, for long the only Gospel known to the Eastern Christians and greatly revered, was eventually condemned by the West as heretical.

THE SASSANIAN CHALLENGE

With the coming of the Sassanian dynasty the Christians soon found themselves in a changing and less favourable environment.

It is impossible to estimate their numbers but we know that they formed a substantial minority of the population and on the whole were well educated and famous for their skill in medicine and the sciences.

Ardeshir, founder of the Sassanian dynasty, was the grandson of Sasan, the *mobed* or priest in charge of the important fire temple at Istakr near Persepolis. The Zoroastrian hierarchy consisted of *mobeds*, who were in charge of an area with numerous lesser clergy under them, and a *mobed-mobedan* or High Priest. As time went on, the power of the religious hierarchy greatly increased and they and the hereditary nobles and lesser rulers were constant sources of concern to the Shah-in-Shah or King. By 237 Ardeshir had made inroads into the Roman frontier provinces and had captured the important fortresses of Haran and Nisibis. The war continued and in 258–9 Ardeshir's successor, Shapur I, pushed west as far as Antioch, beseiged Edessa, and even captured the unfortunate Roman Emperor Valerian.

The result of this successful campaign was that vast numbers of prisoners were brought into Persia. Many of these were Christians, including, it is said, Demetrius, Bishop of Antioch. The prisoners were settled near the small village of Beit Lapat in Khuzistan and were ordered by the King to build a new town, Gondishapur, afterwards to become a famous centre of learning. There is no doubt that many of the doctors and other learned men who made the university of Gondishapur famous were Christians.

The first figure in the Christian Church who emerges clearly is Papa, who became Bishop of Seleucia-Ctesiphon (the capital of the Empire) around 300. His importance lies in the fact that he tried to define the limits of the various dioceses, to regularise the method of appointing bishops and to bring them into some sort of federation, which would acknowledge the supremacy of the see of which he was bishop. Naturally enough, he met with considerable opposition, notably from Miles, Bishop of Susa. Miles, who was born near present-day Tehran, was a convert from Zoroastrianism and as Wigram puts it 'began to show that combination of devotion, zeal, quarrelsomeness and restlessness which makes him so typical a son of his nation'. After quarrelling with his diocese he went on a pilgrimage to Jerusalem and Egypt. On his return he attended the episcopal synod convened to discuss the reforms of Papa. During the synod the argument between Miles and Papa became so heated that the elderly Papa had a stroke and had to retire temporarily from his post, leaving his reforms uncompleted.

THE PERSECUTION UNDER SHAPUR

In 323 the Emperor Constantine issued the Edict of Toleration at Milan. This meant the end of persecution for Christians in the Roman Empire and the nominal if not actual acceptance of Christianity as its official religion. In his Church history Eusebius relates that Constantine wrote a letter to King Shapur II congratulating him on his good treatment of the Christians in his kingdom and rejoicing in the continued growth of the Church in Persia. There is indeed much evidence that in the early years of Shapur's reign – at least until the death of Constantine in 337 – the King was disposed to treat the Christians well. All this changed, however, when Shapur felt himself strong enough to challenge Rome and to demand back the five provinces ceded to Galerius in 297. Constantine, for whom the Persians had great personal respect, died just before the war broke out. His death no doubt encouraged the Persians to treat the Christians with manifest mistrust and to brand them as traitors. In 340 the King informed Simon Bar Sabbae, the Bishop of Seleucia-Ctesiphon (or the Catholicos as he was called), that henceforth he must collect double the previous tax from the Christians. The Catholicos refused to consent to such an unjust imposition. He was summoned to the court and given a final chance to agree. He again refused saying: 'I am no tax-collector but a shepherd of the Lord's flock.' On Good Friday, 17 April 341, he and about 100 other Christians, including many clergy and some monks and nuns, were put to death. The long martyrdom of the Persian Christians had begun. This persecution lasted for almost forty years with scarcely any remission, and was borne with remarkable fortitude. Apostacies were few and the early Martyrologies are full of accounts of torture and sufferings borne with that courage and loyalty which Persians have always shown themselves capable of in any cause to which they have given their allegiance.

The accusations against the Christians that gave rise to the persecution are summed up in the King's official rescript authorising its commencement. These Nazarenes 'inhabit our country and share the sentiments of our enemy Caesar' – words which have echoed in the ears of Persian Christians down the centuries even to the present day.

The desire of the Church to become fully national helps to explain a good deal of its future history. The problem of reconciling the supranational claims of Christianity with the just claim that the Church in Persia must be truly Persian has always puzzled the Church; and the Christians in Persia today are still confronted with it.

Many refugees from Shapur's persecution fled the country and took refuge in Nisibis. Here James of Nisibis, on his return from the Council of Nicaea in 325, had opened a theological school. In 363 Shapur regained Nisibis from the Emperor Jovian and the school moved to Edessa and with it a number of Persians. According to Cardinal Tisserant, the Persians being Indo-Europeans were especially active in translating Greek works of all kinds into Syriac. While these exiles were preparing themselves for their return home as soon as the persecution ended, the see of Seleucia-Ctesiphon remained empty for nearly forty years (346–83), Papa's three successors, Simon, Shahdust and Barbashemin, having all suffered martyrdom.

REORGANISATION OF THE CHURCH

During the reigns of the next three Kings, Ardeshir II, Shapur III and Bahram IV, the persecution gradually lost momentum and the two latter monarchs were comparatively tolerant. When Yezdgerd I became King in 399 the Roman Emperor Arcadius sent an embassy to offer him his congratulations. The head of the embassy was Marouta, Bishop of Maypherqat, the Martyropolis of Byzantine writers. It was thought that since he was of Mesopotamian origin he might be more acceptable to the Persian King than a Byzantine. In addition he was a skilful physician and the King was glad to make use of his services. Marouta pleaded successfully on behalf of the oppressed Christians. He also helped in the reorganisation of the Church, which after all these years of persecution was in a state of considerable disarray. A synod was held and Qayumma, who was Bishop of Seleucia-Ctesiphon, was asked to resign in favour of Isaac, a younger and more able man (and a relative of the previous bishop Tomarsa). Qayumma was old and was probably glad to make a younger man responsible for such an arduous task. Isaac, with the help of Marouta, immediately started reorganising the scattered Church. Once more the story is the same : opposition and argument, and underlying it all the deep division between those who wished the Church to have as little contact as possible with the West and those who felt that their links with the West were their best guarantee of safety.

In the winter of 409–10 Marouta again visited Persia: this time as the envoy of some Western bishops, including those of Antioch, Aleppo and Edessa. These bishops had given Marouta letters instructing him to try and reconcile the doctrines of the Eastern and the Western Churches. Isaac co-operated enthusiastically and had the letters translated into Persian for presentation to the Shah-in-Shah. Yezdgerd, whose policy was one of peace at home and abroad, welcomed the suggestion of a reconciliation between East and West and issued an Edict of Toleration similar to that of Constantine some eighty-five years earlier. In so doing he incurred the wrath of the Magian hierarchy and was branded as an apostate and an impious ruler. In fact it would seem that Yezdgerd acted in a remarkably statesmanlike way. He realised that above all the country needed peace both internally and externally and that the pretentions of the *Magi* were a definite threat to the power of the throne and must somehow be diminished.

Forty bishops attended the synod under the chairmanship of the *marzban*, or provincial governor. The meetings began at Seleucia-Ctesiphon on 6 January 410. They adopted the Nicene Creed and the other Canons of the Council of Nicaea. They also settled the dispute over the metropolitan see for Susiana. Other dioceses and their sees were defined and given legal titles. The holder of the see of Seleucia-Ctesiphon was to be 'The Grand Metropolitan and Head of all the Bishops'. Unfortunately, the synod was not as fully representative as it should have been since the metropolitans of Fars and the Gulf Islands, Media (Tabriz), Beit Raziqaye (Rayy near Tehran), Abrashahr (Nishapur) and some others were not present; the reason being given that the distance to Seleucia-Ctesiphon was too great. But one cannot help feeling that it may well have been that they did not like the Westernising tendencies of the synod. The King took an active interest in all the meetings and sent an important court official to deliver his message to the assembly. He also confirmed its decisions and undertook to punish those who did not obey them. So after many years of confusion the Church regained some measure of order and stability. Isaac died in the same year and so was not able to see the fruits of his work. He was succeeded by Ahai,

21

who died in 414. On his death the King nominated Yahballaha, and in 418 he was sent as the Royal Ambassador to Constantinople. At the end of the following year the Emperor replied by sending Acacius, Bishop of Amida, as his ambassador to the Persian court. At Acacius' instigation another synod was held to strengthen the doctrine of the Church and to bring it more into line with the West. Both Yezdgerd and Yahballaha died in 420.

Yezdgerd's protection of the Christians had met with a great deal of opposition as had his friendly policy towards Rome. The Zoroastrian hierarchy were concerned because the Christians had used their new-found freedom to preach openly and to seek for converts and that in the new relaxed atmosphere many had openly confessed their faith. This opposition flared up early in the reign of the new King, Bahram V, and resulted in further persecution. The immediate cause of this outbreak was the ill-advised action of certain Christians in Khuzistan, who, with more zeal than common sense, burnt a fire temple at Hormizd-Ardeshir. The persecution was aimed chiefly at the important clergy and laymen; only a very few denied their faith but many went into exile. In 421 the King asked the Romans to return these fugitives and made this demand a pretext for his attack across the frontier. But his attack was repulsed and in 422 the fighting ceased and agreement was signed between Bahram and the Roman Emperor, stating that in return for the toleration of Zoroastrians in the Roman Empire, Christians would be tolerated in Persia.

After two abortive attempts to find a new Catholicos to succeed Yahballaha, Dadishu was appointed. The intermediary in this case was Samuel, Bishop of Tus, who had gained favour by helping defend Khorassan against the attacks of marauding tribes. The appointment, however, did not go unopposed; by the manœuvres of his enemies Dadishu had to spend some time in prison and was only released after the Emperor Theodosius' Ambassador had intervened. Dadishu was an old man and hoped that when he was released from prison he would be allowed to spend the rest of his days in a monastery. This did not suit the rest of the Church who needed Dadishu's leadership, so in 424 a synod was called at Markabta, and not at the capital Seleucia-Ctesiphon. The reason for this change is uncertain but it may be connected with the thought that, with a persecution just ended, a big Christian gathering in the capital might be unwise, or with the wish to emphasise the inde-

22

pendent nature of the meeting. The synod was attended by the six metropolitans and thirty other bishops. When they assembled they begged Dadishu to continue as head of the Church and they made a declaration of independence, protesting that the Church of the East should no longer refer its quarrels to the West and any matters that the Catholicos could not settle should be referred to the Tribunal of Christ alone. This synod was a landmark in the history of the Church in Persia. It elevated the Catholicos to the status of a Patriarch, thus freeing the Church from the rule of the Patriarch of Antioch under whom they had been until that time. This was the beginning of the process of separation both in organisation and doctrine which was irreversibly completed some sixty years later.

GOD OR MAN?

The Persian Church had escaped the violence of the Arian controversy, which was finally settled at the Council of Nicaea. But it did not escape the next great controversy which shook the Church and caused the East and West finally to separate and go their different ways. The controversy was in many ways more subtle than the Arian dispute. It concerned the nature of Christ, and was an attempt to answer the question : How can divinity and humanity be united in one man and what is the relation between these two natures? The differences were largely a matter of language and ways of thought. Once again we can see Western and non-Western ways of thinking in conflict. It is very difficult for us today to sympathise with those who fought so bitterly and so relentlessly for their own views on this matter. But for the early Fathers, schooled in the subtleties of Greek philosophy and language, it seemed to be a matter of life and death. There is also no doubt that many personal and extraneous factors clouded the issue and obscured the real theological differences, which if they had been charitably and calmly discussed might have been amicably resolved.

The two chief protagonists in the Christological Controversy, as it was called, were Cyril, Bishop of Alexandria (who held what was subsequently to become the orthodox view in the West), and Nestorius, Bishop of Constantinople, holding the Eastern view, prevalent in the Patriarchate of Antioch and so also in the Church in Persia. The views attributed to Nestorius should more properly be attributed to two great theologians of the Antiochene school,

23

Diodore of Tarsus and Theodore of Mopsuestia. In the view of Cyril, the divine and the human nature were both fully present in Jesus, the divine nature having eternally existed as a hypostatic distinction in the eternal Godhead. These two natures remained distinct in Jesus, united but not unified; this position is known as dyophysite, that is having two natures. The view of Theodore of Mopsuestia erred in over-emphasising the human nature of Jesus which was somehow indwelt by divine spirit. The two natures were distinct but the union between the divine and the human was progressive and not completed until the Ascension. This view also was dyophysite. A third view allegedly held by the present-day Armenian Church was that the two natures, divine and human, united to become one; this view is known as monophysitism. A modern Armenian scholar, Dr John Hananian, has explained the Armenian view on monophysitism thus: 'the formula adopted by the Armenian Church is identical with the Ephesian formula of St Cyril of Alexandria, that is "one nature united in the Word Incarnate" and is absolutely dissimilar to the one proposed by Eutyches.' Readers who are not theologians will no doubt find these distinctions too subtle and not of vital importance; it should be remembered, however, that even today theologians dispute whether Cyril was really a monophysite or a dyophysite and that the argument still continues, albeit peacefully.

Nestorius brought matters to a head when, soon after his appointment to the see of Constantinople, he preached against applying the expression 'Mother of God' to the Blessed Virgin Mary. Instead he wished to use the expression 'Mother of Christ'. The West claimed that by using such an expression Nestorius was implying that Mary was the mother of a 'mere man'. Nestorius retorted that by calling her 'Mother of God' the West was implying that the Godhead had a human mother. Both were right and both surely were wrong.

In 431 the Emperor was persuaded to call an ecumenical council at Ephesus to settle these differences. The council was opened on 22 June by Cyril, in spite of the fact that many of the Eastern bishops and supporters of Nestorius had not yet arrived. Four days later the Oriental contingent arrived and refused to join Cyril's council. Instead they formed a council of their own and duly deposed and excommunicated Cyril; Cyril and his group in their turn did the same for Nestorius. On 10–11 July the Roman representatives arrived and sided with Cyril and expressly approved and confirmed his condemnation of Nestorius. So Cyril's views eventually prevailed, but by means which can only be described as grossly unfair. Nestorius was deposed from his see and sent into a bitter and humiliating exile. When they saw which way the wind was blowing, the Eastern bishops under John of Antioch hastened to join the Western party. The fact that doctrinally Cyril and his followers had the balance of truth on their side cannot be held to justify their tactics nor their lack of charity. These proceedings must have strengthened the Persian Church's view that Antioch was fundamentally pro-Western and so unlikely to sympathise with, or understand, their aspirations.

THE PARTING OF THE WAYS

In 449 another council was held at Ephesus. The whole proceedings were so outrageously 'rigged' and the representatives of Pope Leo so insulted that it is universally known as the *Latrocinium* or Robber Council. In 451 in order to repair the damage done by the Robber Council a further council was held at Chalcedon for a final condemnation of Nestorianism and to complete the victory of Alexandrian, that is to say Western, views.

The Council of Chalcedon was the parting of the ways for Eastern and Western Christianity. As Bishop Stephen Neill has remarked: 'Almost all Church history has been presented exclusively from the Western point of view. After Chalcedon in 451 the Eastern Churches simply ceased to exist' (Neill, *Studies in Church History*, p. 152). By 1000 the evangelisation of Europe was virtually complete and the Church enjoyed a long reign as the state religion and was a most powerful influence in the civilisation and culture of the West. In the East, on the other hand, the Churches very soon had to struggle against the full force of the first great post-Christian religion, Islam, and to struggle for bare survival against the persistent hostility and stagnation of the lands where they had been planted.

THE MARTYRS OF KIRKUK

In speaking of the Council of Chalcedon in 451 we have got a little ahead of our account of affairs in the Church in Persia. In 438 Yezdgerd II succeeded his father Bahram. At first he tolerated the Christians, but after eight years (for reasons which are not altogether

25

clear to us) he turned against them. On 24 and 25 August 446 Christians from a number of provinces, including the bishops, senior clergy and many members of distinguished families, were collected at Karka (modern Kirkuk) and put to death. They met their martyrdom with great courage. The way in which one of the Christian women, Shirin, and her two sons met their death so touched the King's officer in charge of the proceedings that he too confessed faith in Christ and on 25 September was himself crucified. The next year saw the death of the famous martyr, Pethion, who had been a notable evangelist in Western Persia. He had many followers among the important families of the area, including a high-ranking military officer and the chief of police of Shahin. Eventually he was imprisoned and after being tortured for several days was beheaded and his head was exposed on the Royal Road near Kholwan. The persecution extended to Jews and Armenians and was so fierce that it has remained in the minds of Christians up to the present day. The little Christian community in Kirkuk still gathers together year by year to celebrate the faith and courage of their martyred forebears.

THE RAVAGES OF THE WILD BOAR

At this time the state of the Persian Empire and the state of the monarchy in particular, were very unstable. When Yezdgerd died there were two claimants to the throne who reigned as rivals for two years before Piroz (Firuz) proved victorious. He reigned from 456 to 484. For the greater part of his reign his chief adviser was a Christian, Bar Sauma. Bar Sauma was born about 420 and received his education at the famous school of Edessa. He was one of a group of brilliant young Persian students and was given the nickname of 'the wild boar'. He soon made his name as an extreme partisan of Nestorian views, encouraged no doubt by Ibas, the head of the school. In 449, as a result of the Robber Council, Ibas was expelled from the school and Bar Sauma left with him. They both returned to Edessa in 451 when the Council of Chalcedon reversed the decision of the Robber Council.

On the death of Ibas in 457 all his followers were expelled from Edessa and many of them, including Bar Sauma, returned to Persia, where they soon became prominent in the administration and life of the country. Bar Sauma became bishop of the frontier provinces with the metropolitan see of Nisibis. In the same year Babowai was appointed Catholicos. Immediately a great rivalry sprang up between these two prominent and ambitious men. One of the points of difference between them was the question of sacerdotal celibacy, which Babowai tried to enforce and which Bar Sauma opposed – not surprisingly since he himself wished to get married. Babowai was a first-generation convert from Zoroastrianism and like many such, was exceedingly strict and rigid in his outlook. But his position as an apostate from the state religion made him very vulnerable, a fact which Bar Sauma well understood and made use of. Unfortunately for him Babowai made the grave mistake of writing a letter to the Emperor in Constantinople. Bar Sauma arranged for this letter to come into the hands of the King, who objected to it as being treasonable. So in 484 Babowai was condemned to a peculiarly unpleasant form of death : he was suspended by the finger on which he wore the ring he had used to seal the letter, and was left to starve to death. Bar Sauma now felt free to carry on with his schemes; he advised the King to support the schism between East and West, and to use royal troops to compel Christians to adopt the teachings of Nestorius. At least, such is the hostile report put out by monophysite opponents of Bar Sauma.

Piroz died in this same year and Acacius was appointed Catholicos or Patriarch, as he should now be called. Acacius was of the same doctrinal persuasion as Bar Sauma and there should have been no reason why they should quarrel, but quarrel they did. A synod was called in the following year, 485, at Beit d'Edrai. Bar Sauma was rejected by the Church as a whole and his actions of the previous year were condemned. The next year another meeting was held and this synod is generally held to mark the final break of the Church in Persia with the West. The struggles between Bar Sauma and Acacius continued until the latter's death in 496. In the years that followed, a superficial uniformity was achieved by persecuting those bishops who still professed monophysite views. This was done with the assistance of the new King, Kavad, who arranged for the arrest and condemnation of those who did not conform.

Shortly before the reign of Kavad (484–531), an extraordinary heresy arose in Zoroastrianism under a leader named Mazdak. The Mazdakites practised a form of communism including sharing wives and families, or so their enemies alleged. It was undoubtedly a revolt by the less fortunate classes against the rigid caste system

27

of the *Magi* and their ruthless persecution of unorthodox opinions of all kinds. About this time we read of a Zoroastrian priest called Kartir who was very active in establishing fire temples and suppressing the heresies of Christians, Jews, Buddhists, Hindus, Nazoreans and Manichaeans. This list of heresies shows how wide the range of other religions was at this time. Kavad was succeeded by the greatest of the Sassanian monarchs, Khosro I, known as Anushiravan, the Great Soul, who was also and justly granted the title of 'the Great'. He reigned until 579 and during his long reign Persia enjoyed a new period of stability and well-being such as she had not known for very many years and was not to enjoy again for an even longer period. Khosro Anushiravan was a great patron of the arts and sciences, and scholars and learned men from East and West were welcomed at his court.

REVIVAL UNDER MAR ABA

Between Acacius, who died in 496, and Mar Aba who became Patriarch in 540, the Church had a series of leaders of inferior quality whose lives and quarrels need not detain us. Aba was a man of a very different calibre, a man of great holiness, scholarship and administrative ability. He was a convert from Zoroastrianism and in early life had entered the government service and risen to the important post of secretary to a provincial governor. After his conversion he spent some time studying in Alexandria and Constantinople. On his return he went to Nisibis where he wanted to lead the life of a solitary hermit, but he was persuaded by the bishop to become a teacher. He gained such a reputation for sanctity and learning that when the patriarchal see became vacant in 540 (or possibly 537) he was appointed without dissension. One of his first acts was to visit various dioceses to settle differences and to heal old wounds. In all this he was outstandingly successful. It is a tribute to his greatness and patriotic spirit that he gained the friendship and trust of the King. This friendship was to stand him in good stead when the *mobeds*, concerned at the success of the Christians in drawing many to them, brought accusations against Mar Aba, which the King very reluctantly had to take notice of. But instead of allowing him to be condemned to death he exiled Aba to Azerbaijan, where he continued to administer, to encourage and to inspire his Church. Eventually after seven years the *mobeds* hired an apostate Christian to assassinate him, but the wretched man was unable to carry out his task. With great courage Aba decided to return to the capital, much to the astonishment of the King who, on meeting him, asked him what he was doing. Aba explained that he had perfect trust in the King's justice and if the King wanted him to be executed he would consent, but he would not consent to be executed without a trial. Once more accusations were brought against him and he was almost put to death. The King agreed to his being held in prison but gave orders that he was on no account to be killed. Finally the King's son by a Christian woman raised a revolt in Khuzistan in which Aba was thought to have had a hand. He pleaded to be allowed to go there and show his loyalty by pacifying the rebels. Permission was granted and he was successful, but the effort was too much for him and worn out by all his exertions he died in 552. Khosro Anushira-van continued to rule until 579 when he was succeeded by his son, Hormizd IV, who was by no means an unworthy successor to his great father. But the days of the Sassanians were numbered; in the space of forty years, ten Kings came and went. The kingdom was exhausted physically and economically by the prolonged wars on its eastern and western frontiers. The state religion had become increas-ingly oppressive and out of touch with the needs and aspirations of the bulk of the population. The Church shared in the national decay. Between the death of Mar Aba in 552 and 650, eight Patriarchs followed one another, with a gap of twenty years between 608 and 628 when the position was vacant. None of these leaders was outstanding in any way.

Things were ripe for a change and this came when the Arabs, bursting out of their bare peninsula, swept westwards into the Fertile Crescent. In a remarkably short space of time Persia too succumbed to the invaders. In 632 the Sassanian army was destroyed and its general, Rustam, was killed; by the end of that year the whole of the Mesopotamian plain had submitted. The heartlands of Iran were next invaded and in 642 the final battle was fought at Niha-vand. The invading armies spread rapidly in all directions taking Hamadan, Isfahan, Kerman and Khorassan in quick succession. The wretched Persian King, Yezdgerd III, fled northwards and was finally murdered in Merv by a traitor in his own army.

Chapter Three

THE PERSIAN CHURCH AT THE COMING OF ISLAM

Before going any further in relating the history of the Church in Persia, it is worth pausing for a moment to consider what kind of Church it was.

Most of the evidence which has come down to us is naturally concerned with the synods and councils of the whole Church and the official actions and reactions of its leaders. Some evidence is available about the widespread monasticism of the Church, and a good deal about its remarkable missionary expansion. But what is almost entirely lacking is information about the daily life of the ordinary Church member. Perhaps the most striking feature of the early Church was its predominantly monastic character. If we take as our guide the writings of the Persian sage, Aphraates, who wrote during the middle of the fourth century, we find that the Christians of his time were divided into two groups, the Bar Qiyama and the Penitents. The Bar Qiyama, a Syriac term meaning 'Sons and Daughters of the Covenant', is often taken to mean monks and nuns, and the term Penitents to mean catechumens awaiting baptism. If we follow Professor Burkitt's interpretation of these terms it would seem that the Sons and Daughters of the Covenant were in fact the baptised laity, and that baptism was reserved for those who were prepared to lead an ascetic and celibate life, renouncing the world. Those who were not prepared to do so were not admitted to baptism and possibly not to the Sacraments either. Recent research has cast some doubt on the absolute validity of this opinion but it seems to be still substanially upheld. The early Church in Persia, faced as it was with a strong and hostile state religion that inspired long and cruel persecutions of the Christians, naturally tended to reject the world and to hope for better things in the world to come, to be obtained by rigorous self-denial in this one. Thus a monastic style of life was held up as the pattern for Christians. Aphraates in his discourse on the Sacraments makes no mention of marriage; indeed, as Burkitt remarks, such a thing in his system would have been quite irrational, like a sacrament of usury or military service.

> The Christian community with all its privileges and blessings is, on this theory, restricted to celibates who have as much as possible withdrawn from the world; the mass of the people stand outside. Not only Art, Science and Politics but also the Hearth and the Home are shut out from the province of religion (Burkitt, *Early Eastern Christianity*, p. 140).

Obviously such an extreme view could not prevail for ever, and as the Church became more accepted and powerful the rules were relaxed, and by the middle of the fifth century marriage ceased to be a bar to baptism. The Sons and Daughters of the Covenant, however, remain the backbone of the Church. It would seem that a wide variety of types of settlement existed. Some were monasteries, founded on the Egyptian pattern, in wild and inaccessible places. In Persia this meant for the most part on the tops and sides of rocky mountains, where some of the monks could live in natural caves. Others would be in a village, grouped round the church with members either living in their own homes or in simple stone dwellings. Until the reforms of Abraham of Kashkhar in the middle of the sixth century, there was a good deal of laxity and a blurring of distinctions between the Bar Qiyama and the rest of the community. The rule, when it was faithfully observed, was a strict one, but one feature essential to Western monasticism was not mentioned in the original rules nor in the reformed rules of Abraham – and that was, obedience. The seven canonical hours of prayer were observed (later reduced to four); only one meal a day was taken, at noon, consisting of bread and vegetables; flesh was forbidden. The monks spent their time either doing scholastic tasks in the monastery or gardening outside it. Monasteries were nominally under the control of the local bishop who controlled their goods and money, but within the monastery the monks were strong individualists, who did more or less what they liked. Celibacy, poverty, fasting, prayer, study and silence were insisted on. Such an ascetic and world-renouncing ideal, however attractive it was for the hardpressed Christian minority, was not at all attractive to the Zoroastrian majority. As Professor Zaehner says :

In principle Zoroastrianism was bitterly opposed to asceticism as being a blasphemy against life . . . Zoroastrianism like Islam only praises poverty in its less characteristic moments, for its whole ethos is one of productivity, of giving *and* receiving and of growth . . . growth in virtue on the one hand and growth in wealth on the other; and it is doubtful whether any other religion could define 'man's perfect desire' as being 'a desire to amass worldly goods as much as to further righteousness thereby'.

Such a religion had a natural appeal in Iran, where water is scarce and a largely agricultural population know that they must produce plentifully or die. Islam inherited this situation and was in essence equally averse to asceticism and religious separatism, being very much an egalitarian religion without distinction between lay and religious, and very much the religion of moderation.

One other point about the Church needs to be mentioned and that is that the language of the Church was Syriac, which was not the language of the mass of the people. In the *Chronique de Seert* we read about various efforts being made in the fifth century to translate into Pahlavi religious works and even discourses, canticles and hymns to be recited in Church, and we know that the canons of the Church, at least in the province of Fars, were written in Persian under the metropolitan Simon in 670. But, basically, the language of the Church was foreign to the people and not understood. When, under Islam, the Persian language became a means of maintaining the national identity, the failure of the Church to adopt it as its language for worship must inevitably have militated against it. So great was the Persian affection for their language that *The Shahnameh*, the great Persian epic by Firdausi (completed in 1010), is said to contain not more than four or five per cent of Arabic words, and presumably not a single Syriac word.

Chapter Four

THE COMING OF ISLAM:
THE SHADOW OF THE GHETTO

For a subject people, a change of masters often raises hopes that it will be a change for the better, but in fact it seldom is. At least some of the Christians in the Persian Empire hoped that the Arabs might be an improvement on the Sassanians. The Christians of the Mesopotamian basin, as opposed to those of the Persian highlands, were Semites with a Semitic language and they believed that the invaders would give them preferential treatment. Shortly before the death of Muhammad in 632, the Persian Patriarch sent Bishop Gabriel of Maysan to the Prophet to ask for this protection for the Christians in the Arabian peninsula. Apparently a charter was granted, known as the Covenant of the Prophet (copies of it are preserved in the Monastery of St Catherine on Mt Sinai), but even if it was not a later forgery, it seems to have been of little value. If a group was to receive preferential treatment from the invaders it was necessary that they should be both Arab from the Arabian peninsula and Muslim. The Christian Arabs of Hira found this out when they were expected to billet the invaders in their churches, which were sometimes desecrated by being used as stables.

From the beginning, the Arab policy was one of divide and rule. They gave special treatment to Jews and Christians (mainly Semites), whom they called People of the Book, that is those who had written scriptures which Muslims, at least in part, accepted. The Zoroastrians who were mainly Aryan were not so classed and were thus placed over and against the Semites. (Later, for fiscal reasons, the Zoroastrians were also classed as People of the Book). Some of the Arab Christians from Mesopotamia fought alongside the invaders when they attacked the Persian plateau in the campaigns of 636–8.

When the initial fighting was over, the Arabs settled down to rule their vast new dominions. Naturally enough they did not want to disturb any more of the existing administrative organisation than was absolutely necessary. So far as was possible they left things unchanged, adapting existing institutions to conform with nascent Islamic law. The Christians, too, for a while at least, retained their former status. But they remained a subject people, *dhimmis*, second-class citizens allowed to keep their religion only in return for the payment of a swingeing poll-tax. They were an alien body in the commonwealth, fenced in by sumptuary laws, prohibitions and dis-abilities – all of which would immediately be removed if they opted for Islam. Many nominally adopted the faith of Islam, but they seemed to have had no such secret source of strength as supported the Jewish *Marranos* in similar circumstances. Those who could be of use to the conquerors, either as merchants or because of their skill in medicine and science, were more likely to find ways and means of mitigating their disabilities and so to be resigned to their equivocal position. Throughout this period we find confessed Christians occupying important positions in the court and even sometimes in the provincial administrations. As monks were exempt from the poll-tax and were generally left alone, it was the ordinary Church members who tended to adopt the new faith in the greatest numbers, thus cutting the Church off from its contact with the general public.

Apart from the disabilities imposed on individuals, the Church as a corporate body was also severely limited. It was forbidden to build new churches in towns or large villages, although old buildings could be repaired. Al Baladhuri tells us that among the conditions made after the surrender of Edessa were : Christians must no longer publicly strike clappers (the alternative to bells, widely used in the Eastern Church); they must not openly celebrate Easter Monday, nor must they display the Cross in public. At different periods various other cramping regulations were imposed on the Church.

THE PERSIAN CONQUEST OF ISLAM

Professor Richard Frye in his fascinating book, *The Heritage of Persia*, calls his last chapter 'The Persian Conquest of Islam', and there is a profound truth underlying this paradox. At the coming of Islam, Persia had already had a very long history and was the heir to a great and highly developed culture. The Arabs had prac-tically no history and very little culture. In 661, after the inevitable and bloody internal quarrels among the Arab factions, the first

Ommayad caliph succeeded Ali and life in the newly-conquered territories began to settle down. But the Ommayad caliphs were far from being securely in power. The conquest of Persia was by no means complete; the farther east one went, the less was the caliph's rule apparent. The second caliph, Yazid, was particularly hated and is to this day universally execrated in Persia for having killed the martyr Hussein and for his sacrilegious behaviour in Medina and Mecca.

In 747 Abu'l Abbas al-Saffah, whose name is known to every Persian schoolboy, raised the black standard of revolt in Eastern Persia. This uprising had strong Persian nationalist overtones. Two years later, Abbas, the first of a new dynasty to be known as the Abbasids, pronounced the traditional homily in the mosque at Kufa and so became the new caliph. Although the new dynasty was religiously orthodox, it was not so exclusively pro-Arab as its predecessors. Persians, including many Christians, occupied important positions in government and flourished as traders and businessmen. Persian customs were revived, including the old Persian *No Ruz* ceremony celebrating the Spring equinox. For fifty years the important post of vizier, or first minister, was held by members of a Persian family, descendants of a high priest from the Buddhist monastery of No Bahar near Balkh. The Abbasids moved their capital from Kufa to the newly-built capital of Baghdad, about fifteen miles up the river from Seleucia-Ctesiphon.

Wars with the Byzantine Empire continued spasmodically; whenever they broke out, the Christians were suspected of being friendly with the enemy, as they had been under the Sassanians; a suspicion which may well have been justified on occasions. As a result many Christians crossed the border into the Byzantine Empire and a large group settled in Sinope on the Black Sea.

OPENINGS AND RESTRICTIONS

During the Patriarchate of Hannayeshu II (774–8), the seat of the Patriarchate was moved to Baghdad but the old title was retained. Hannayeshu's successor was Patriarch Timothy, one of the outstanding men of his time. Timothy I (779–823) can be said to typify a Persian Church leader of this time. He was extremely worldly and not above giving or taking a bribe. Although he showed small signs of spirituality, he was zealous for the well-being and good name of

the Church, which he administered very efficiently. He was devoted
to the cause of education, which he considered of prime importance.
In counselling a prospective bishop he advised him to 'take care of
the schools with all your heart. Remember that the school is the
mother and nurse of the sons of the Church.' The fact that so many
Christians were well educated enabled them (like the Copts under
the Fatimids in Egypt) to take leading positions as scribes and
secretaries in the court and in the government. The Caliph Ma'mun
(813–33) founded an institution of higher education known as the
House of Knowledge (Beit al Hekma). Its most famous head was a
Christian scholar called Abu Zayd Hunain, the first of a family
of scholars, all of whom held positions of importance in the institution. Hunain, who was well read in Greek science and philosophy,
translated over 100 works into Arabic and also wrote a number of
works on religion. Towards the end of the Abbasid period the ban
on the building of churches was relaxed and we hear of new
churches being constructed, such as that built by Cyprian of
Nisibis, which cost 56,000 gold dinars.

As Professor Tritton has pointed out (*Encyclopedia of Islam*
(1936), article on Nasara) relations between Muslims and
Christians were often friendly. A Muslim poet boasted that he never
wrote poems about the wife of a Muslim or a Christian. There is
also no doubt that many Christians flourished for a while. A Muslim
doctor complained that he could not get any patients in an unhealthy
season because he spoke good Arabic and not the dialect of
Gondishapur and did not dress in rich silks. But as Professor Tritton
concludes:

> In spite of all this, the stigma remained. The humiliating regula-
> tions, the need for constant watchfulness, the constant recourse to
> intrigue and influence to circumvent the law, the segregation of
> the religious minorities or *dhimmis* in many cities, inevitably
> sapped their morale. Still more serious were their legal disabilities,
> there could be no true justice for the *dhimmi* . . . nor could there
> be any permanent social relationship in the absence of inter-
> marriage. It is not surprising therefore that the Christian com-
> munities of the East gradually dwindled, not only in numbers but
> in vitality and moral tone' (Tritton, op. cit.).

There is no doubt that the rise of Islam posed enormous problems
for the Persian Church and its apologists, and indeed for the whole

of Christendom. How did it come about that a new monotheistic religion having so much in common with Christianity could arise and be so obviously successful? Was Muhammad to be regarded as a heretic, an imposter, a self-deluded man, or a true prophet? The debate still goes on and it is interesting to find that a modern writer, Jean Guitton, echoes the thoughts of an early critic of Islam, John of Damascus, by treating it as a Christian heresy (Guitton, *Great Heresies and Church Councils*, pp. 99–121).

These doubts, together with the vigour, simplicity and military success of the new religion, were a great shock to the worldly and theologically insipid Nestorian Church and forced it on to the defensive. In addition, the rigorous attitude of Islam towards Muslims who wished to apostasise did not encourage converts to come forward, nor the Church to look for them. The old pre-Islamic conviction was that religion and nationality were closely allied. The notion that to be a Persian you had to be a Zoroastrian was replaced by : to be a Persian you had to be a Muslim. Thus no place was left for Persian Christians. Nevertheless, the Church as we shall see still had considerable vitality. The restless energy of the monks, who were ever prone to wander, was directed to evangelism outside the cramping confines of the caliphate, into those regions in the East where they felt free and were gladly received.

Chapter Five

THE MISSIONARY EXPANSION
OF THE CHURCH

The period between the end of the effective rule of the Abbasid Caliphate in Iran and the coming of the Mongols was one of great storm and stress in the Islamic world and not least in Persia. There, the power eventually fell into the hands of two dynasties, the Samanids in the north-east and the Buwahids in the south. Both were energetic and enlightened rulers and the Buwahids promoted many Christians to positions of considerable importance in their administration.

This period also saw the intensification of the split between the orthodox Sunnis and the heretical adherents of Ali, notably the Ismailis, whose radical wing were to become the Assassins, and the more conventional Shia, whose brand of Islam, moulded and transformed by Persian thought and culture, was eventually to become the prevailing orthodoxy in Iran. From the start, the Shia was an opposition party; there is no doubt that in much of its mystical and eschatological thinking, Shia Islam was strongly influenced by Christian ideas. Ali is sometimes claimed as divine and Hussein, the martyr, becomes a Christ-like figure who can act as an intermediary between man and God. The doctrine of the twelfth Imam, who will return one day in final judgement, echoes closely the eschatological hopes of the early Christian Church.

Towards the end of the tenth century, Turkish tribes from Transoxiana (who for long had provided mercenaries for the Caliphate) accepted Islam, and half a century later crossed the Oxus, flooding into Persia and moving westwards into Turkey. The most important of these tribes was the Seljuk, whose members were orthodox Sunnis; so once more the Persians found themselves under alien rule. Alp-Arsalan, one of the greatest Persian Seljuk rulers, defeated the Byzantine Emperor in 1073 at the battle of Manzikert, thus alerting the West to the threat of Islam; an awareness which resulted in the Crusades. Naturally enough, Alp-Arsalan did not take kindly to the presence of Christians in his dominions and we read that he gave orders that iron collars should be fixed round the necks of all Christians who refused to adopt Islam. Many other restrictions were placed on Christians by Muslim fanatics, with the result that they became increasingly depressed and their numbers and influence gradually declined.

Most of the history of the Christian Church – even in the period before the Seljuk invasion – is to be found in its expansion outside the confines of Persia proper, as it carried the Gospel with great zeal and pertinacity to the farthest confines of India and China and penetrated deeply into Central Asia.

PERSIAN MISSIONS TO CENTRAL ASIA

The expansion of Christianity into Central Asia from the north of Persia was rapid and the faith soon took root among the migratory and semi-migratory tribes of Mongols, Turks and Tartars. By 424 Rayy and Nishapur in Northern Persia, Merv in Russian Turkmenistan and Herat in Afghanistan, were all episcopal sees and centres from which teams of Persian monks were sent out on evangelistic journeys. In 498 Kavad, the Sassanian King, took refuge with the Hephthalite Huns and found that there were many Christians amongst them who were willing to help him. Thus when he returned to power he tended to favour Christians. These Huns are said to have been evangelised by a Nestorian monk, John of Resh-Aina, of the monastery of Ishakanai, who taught them the art of writing, and a layman, Thomas the Tanner, who lived with them for thirty years. The *Chronique de Seert* also tells us that an Armenian bishop spent some years among the Turks as an agricultural missionary, teaching them how to grow vegetables and how to plant corn. In 539 the Hephthalite Huns asked the Catholicos Aba I to consecrate a bishop for them, thus indicating the presence of a considerable Christian community. Shortly before this, a bishop of Arran (the Armenian Aghwank, now Soviet Azerbaijan) set out with six companions – four monks and two laymen – on a missionary journey to another tribe of Huns in Transoxiana; and in the middle of the seventh century Elie, Metropolitan of Merv, himself worked as a missionary among Turkish tribes in the same area.

But the biggest outreach was made under the Catholicos Timothy I by monks from the monastery at Beit Aba. In 781 Timothy writes that yet another ruler of a Turkish tribe had become a Christian and that he had consecrated a bishop for him. He also mentions consecrating a bishop for Tibet and speaks of missionary journeys being made to India and China. About this time, also, the principality of Kashkhar became Christian and its first Christian prince was baptised Sergius. Later, in the twelfth century, when Muslims invaded this area, they were opposed by Christian troops under a Christian governor of Aksu, vassal of a Christian prince of Khotan.

In 1009 Abdishu, Metropolitan of Merv, wrote to the Nestorian Patriarch saying that there had been a mass movement to Christianity among the Keraites, an important tribe living in western Mongolia, to the south-east of Lake Baikal. He estimated that 200,000 souls had been added to the Church. A similar movement took place among the Onguts from the Yellow River.

MISSIONARY EXPANSION TO INDIA

Traditionally there have always been two routes east from Persia : the sea route in the south down the Persian Gulf to the Indian Ocean and onwards, and the land route across the north of the country. In pre-Christian times the ships of the Babylonian Empire had pioneered the sea voyage to India, and by the beginning of the Christian era this was a well-travelled trade route. When Christianity became established in the Persian Empire, Christians, either as missionaries or traders, spread the faith up and down both sides of the Persian Gulf. It was with some of these Christian colonies that Muhammad had contact. The Island of Socotra, an important trading post off the south coast of the Arabian Peninsula and with a mixed population of Greeks, Arabs, Persians and Hindus, soon became a centre of Christianity and was granted a bishop by the Catholicos Sabr-Ishu (1064–72). Two hundred years later, when Marco Polo called there, he still found a flourishing Christian community.

It is also by means of the sea route that Christianity reached India. The Byzantine traveller Cosmas Indicopleustes who travelled in Ethiopia, Arabia and India in about 520 writes that Ceylon 'had a church of Persian Christians who have settled there and a Presbyter who is appointed from Persia and a Deacon and a complete ecclesiastical ritual' (Indicopleustes, *The Christian Topography*, trans. McCrindle, p. 365) but this seems to have been a group of Persian Christian merchants with a chaplain, rather than a missionary outpost. Missionaries may well have been there and gone farther, for Indicopleustes also tells us that 'Ceylon was much frequented by ships from all over India and from Persia and Ethiopia, and likewise sends out many of its own'. We know that it was a staging post in the maritime trade between China and Rome, where the merchants exchanged their goods and carried them home in their own vessels. However, he did find a genuine indigenous Christian community at Quilon on the Malabar coast. These were the Christians who traced their origin back to the missionary endeavours of St Thomas the Apostle. The Christians in the province of Fars and in the Persian Gulf always felt a particular affinity with these Indian Christians and on occasion associated themselves with them as a means of resisting the claims of the Catholicos of Seleucia-Ctesiphon. It may well be that there was considerable coming and going between the two areas and Indian Christians may well have settled on the Persian coast. This would explain a curious passage in the *Acta S. Maris* (the life of the semi-legendary St Mari) where it is recorded that the saint penetrated from Edessa into the province of Fars 'until he smelt the smell of St Thomas' – in other words, until he met with some Christians from India.

Apart from the Malabar-coast evidence, there are few indications of early Christianity in India. A number of crosses have been found bearing Pahlavi inscriptions. Two famous identical crosses are those at Milapore on the Coromandel coast near Madras and that preserved in an ancient church in Kottayam. Documents have also been discovered dating from between 700 and 824, granting special privileges to Christians. That of 824 is written in Tamil, Pahlavi and Arabic. They would appear to have been occasioned by a sudden influx of Christians from Persia (similar to the influx of Zoroastrians a few years later, which gave rise to the Parsee community of India which survives to this day). The Christians, among whom there were many natives as well as Persians, were granted what practically amounts to the status of a caste. The main centre of this community was the important town of Cranganore. There are many gaps in the history of these Christians. But they survived – often in poverty and ignorance – and today, in spite of the efforts of Protestant and Roman Catholic missionaries, the ancient Church still has its adherents.

41

THE NESTORIAN CHURCH IN CHINA

As has been said, the contact between the West and China was a well-established fact by the end of the first century AD – both by land and by sea. At this time the main point of contact between the West and China was the great city of Antioch in Syria, the seat of the mother Church of all Eastern Christians. The mutual contacts made there may have resulted in some inklings of the new religion penetrating to China very early indeed.

The main route of penetration was the land route in the north. Indeed, for centuries missionaries from Persia were making contact with the various tribes of Turks, Huns and Tartars who roamed the steppes and the vast area between the Oxus and the frontiers of China. Tribes of Turks helped establish the Tang dynasty in China; it is during this dynasty that Christianity nearly became one of the national religions of China.

Sian Fu, which is now the capital of the Shensi province, is one of the great historical towns of China and for many centuries (under various names) was the capital. Lying as it does close to the junction of the Wei and Ching Rivers with the Yellow River, it is a great centre of trade and the terminal point of innumerable caravan routes. It has also been for long periods a great centre of culture and learning. Under the Emperor Tai Tsung (the second ruler of the Tang dynasty) it became an international centre where Buddhist, Zoroastrian and Manichaean as well as Christian monks were welcomed. After the Arab invasion of Persia, the last Sassanian King took refuge here for a time and his son lived on here in exile until 707.

Most, but not all of our knowledge of the early progress of Christianity in China, where it was known as The Luminous Way, is derived from the famous Sian Fu stone. This famous monument was discovered in 1625 and brought to the notice of the Western world by Jesuit missionaries then working in China. An account of it was published by the Jesuit Athanasius Kircher in his book *China Monumentis . . . illustrata*, published in Amsterdam in 1667. For a long time the authenticity of the stone was doubted; Voltaire made fun of it in the fourth of his Chinese and Indian Letters. Later scholars have also cast doubts on its authenticity, but the most modern consensus of opinion is that there is no possible doubt as to its genuineness. In 1907 it was again brought to the attention of the Western world by the exertions of a Danish journalist, Fritz von

Holm, who, having failed to buy it, had an exact replica made of it, which is now in the Vatican Museum. He also wrote a book about it which was widely read.

The monument is a block of black limestone a little over 9 feet high, $3\frac{1}{3}$ feet wide and about 1 foot thick. The original, as far as is known, is still in China. When the church of St Simon the Zealot was built in Shiraz in 1937 the priest in charge, the Reverend Norman Sharp, had the happy idea of having a facsimile of the headstone of the monument made and placed in the church as a fitting memorial to Persia's great Christian past. Another exact replica was erected in October 1911 on the choicest of three sites offered by the Lord Abbot of Koyosan, the chief Buddhist sanctuary in Japan, which Kobo Daishi founded in 816 after visiting Sian Fu (see Gordon, *Asian Cristology and the Mahayana*, pp. 224–5).

The stone was originally erected in 781 in the enclosure of the Christian monastery founded in 638 by order of the Emperor Tai Tsung in a western suburb of his capital Sian Fu. The purpose of the monument seems to have been to commemorate an annual reunion held in 779 at the expense of a notable Christian Yi-Issu or Yazd Bozid. The inscription which is on all sides of the stone consists of 1,900 Chinese characters and about 50 Syriac words and some 70 Syriac names with the Chinese transliterations. The text gives a brief outline of the doctrine of Christianity and of its history in China up to that time. One Persian word is found on it, *yaksam-bun*, denoting Sunday (*yekshambeh*). Full details of the inscription can be found in the books by von Holm, Saeki and Foster (see Bibliography).

Briefly, the history which can be derived from this stone and from the Chinese annals of the Tang dynasty is as follows. In 635 the Christian prince of the border state of Khotan sent his son to Sian Fu to take advantage of the educational facilities offered there. In the same year and possibly accompanying the Khotanese prince, a Persian missionary, whose name is given as Alopen, came to the court of the Emperor Tai Tsung. He was received with honour and stayed in the Emperor's palace.

In 638 the emperor issued an Edict of Toleration for the Christians and ordered that a monastery should be built for Alopen and twenty-one monks. The next Emperor, Kao Tsung, was a powerful ruler and extended the boundaries of his Empire to the Oxus; he too honoured and favoured the Christians. On his death, the

43

Dowager Empress Wu Hou, who had been a Buddhist nun, took over the reins of government and in favouring the Buddhists, discriminated against all other religions. Between 698 and 712 the Christians were exposed to a certain amount of trouble and a mob attacked the monastery. However, from 713 to 763 the new religion enjoyed a period of calm and great influence in the government and at court. This was during the reign of the Emperor Hsuang Tsung, a man of great culture, passionately interested in the arts. He founded the famous academy of Hanlin where music, poetry and painting were all studied. The Emperor became infatuated with a beautiful woman and neglected the responsibilities of government, with the result that in 756 he found himself faced with a serious revolt. From then until the end of his reign, the country was shaken by numerous revolts and wars. The Church, led mainly by Yazd Bozid, took a prominent part in the life of the country. Yazd Bozid, who was universally loved and admired for his piety and charity, went on a campaign with the Duke of Kwoh and his willingness to rough it with the simple soldiers greatly endeared him to them. Another Church leader, Adam, gained fame as a calligrapher, an art very highly esteemed in China. It was he who wrote the Sian Fu tablet; he was also the author of numerous books, some of which have survived.

THE DISAPPEARANCE OF THE CHURCH IN CHINA

When in 845 the Church was finally proscribed along with other foreign religions such as Buddhism and Zoroastrianism, it was because they constituted alien enclaves in the country and thousands of monks in their monasteries were living idle and luxurious lives. In times of stress, actions like the suppression of foreign religions can always be taken in order to assist in the re-establishment of a national religion, in this case, Taoism. Under such circumstances the merits of the religion are not so important as the fact that it seems to be foreign.

If we were to sum up the extent and achievement of the Church in China we can see that in times of religious toleration it flourished and exerted a considerable influence on the national life. Some believe that as a result of the contact in China at this time between Buddhism and Christianity we can find traces of Christian influence in Mahayana Buddhism. It is very difficult to make more than a guess as to how widespread the faith was. It would seem certain, however, that there were Christians, sometimes as traders and some-times grouped in monasteries as monks, in the ports and centres of trade along and around the Yellow River. There is no doubt that monks were admired for their skill in science and medicine, but the religion was an exotic growth, one of many strange sects struggling for recognition and one which never took root among the mass of the people. In 981 when the Nestorian Patriarch, Abdishu I, sent monks to China they are reported (by the Muslim historian Abul-faraj) to have found not one single Christian left in China. Saeki believes that the mass of Christians eventually became Muslims or joined a secret society called the Society of the Luminous Pill, whose tenets show distinct traces of Christian doctrine. But some monastic life at least survived for many more years, witness the arrival of the two Chinese monks whose adventures we shall describe later (see pp. 50–51).

Archaeology and palaeography may yet reveal to us facts which will help us to fill in the many gaps in our knowledge. The stone cross with the Pahlavi inscription of Psalm 24, verse 6, which was discovered in 1920 and the manuscripts bought by Japanese scholars about the same time, encourage us to hope that still more may come to light. These manuscripts, which date from the seventh century, are of great interest as they prove conclusively that the Christianity propagated by Alopen and his monks was not a watered-down version of the Gospels but was in every respect worthy and compre-hensive. The Gospels were not then translated in full but the Sermon on the Mount and the Passion narratives were, and the *Gloria in Excelsis Deo* was used as a Chinese hymn of praise long before we had it in any vernacular in the West.

Much has been made of the missionary activity of the West. By a curious coincidence the mission of St Aidan from the holy island of Iona to the pagan kingdom of Northumbria took place in the same year as Alopen's arrival in Sian Fu. The two events deserve equal praise in the history of the Church and it is to the eternal credit of the Persian Church of the early days that it had the same adven-turous devotion and evangelistic zeal that its brothers in the West were showing, although it worked in harder circumstances – both spiritual and material.

THE LEGEND OF ST IVES

One final story of Persian missionary enterprise must not go unmentioned. It has no circumstantial evidence to support it but its legendary origin as an incident in Church history is very old and there is nothing inherently impossible in it. I refer to the legend that a Persian missionary came to England in the sixth or seventh century and settled in the fen country, and that the town of St Ives in Huntingdonshire was named after him. The seventeenth-century poet, Michael Drayton, in his topographical poem 'Poly-Olbion' (1622) describes the event thus:

From Persia led by zeal St Ive this island sought,
And near our eastern fens a fit place finding, taught
The Faith; which place from him alone the name derives
And of that sainted man has since been called St Ives.

Chapter Six

THE DECLINE OF THE NESTORIAN CHURCH AND THE FIRST CONTACTS WITH ROME

The rise to power of the Turkish tribes from Transoxiana, mentioned in the previous chapter, gave rise to a fundamental change in the political situation in the Near East. Till then, only the two powers of East and West had to be reckoned with; now a third force had entered the arena. For 200 years they were courted and feared by both sides. It was not until 1295 when the Il Khan Ghazan Khan with all his army made a solemn profession of Islam that the matter of their allegiance was settled once and for all and the broad lines on which all future diplomacy was to be conducted for a very long time were laid down.

Throughout the twelfth century the battle between East and West, which was also the battle between Christians and Muslims, swayed to and fro – the West generally being on the defensive. The Saracens, under their leader Saladin, a prince of Kurdish origin, seized power in Egypt in 1169 and in 1187 took Jerusalem. The West urgently needed help against these all-powerful opponents. For a long time they had heard rumours of a vast and powerful Christian kingdom under a King known as Prester John situated somewhere in the East. Such a legend was probably based on the undisputed fact that, thanks to the missionary zeal of Persian monks, Christianity was widespread in Central Asia and no less than four tribes there were substantially Christian; but it proved a chimera.

COURTING THE MONGOLS

Religion played no part in Mongol policy and with the rise of Genghiz Khan and his inroads into Europe between 1237 and 1242 (which were carried out with amazing speed and cruelty), it became obvious that there was not much for the West to hope for in that direction. Indeed, in 1238 some opponents of the Mongols, namely the Assassins, came to seek an alliance with Britain, against their common enemy. The English reaction was summed up by the Bishop of Winchester, who asked why they should help either side : 'Let these pagan dogs kill one another', he said, 'and we will build the true Catholic Church on the ruins.'

During the interregnum between the death of Genghiz Khan in 1227 and his grandson's adoption of the title of Il Khan of Persia in 1251, the Papacy was seriously disturbed by the Mongol threat and thought it worth while sending embassies to try and come to terms with them and to see if Christians of Asia could not be mobilised on the side of their co-religionists in the West. As a result of the Council of Lyons in 1245, Pope Innocent IV produced his famous tract *Remedium contra Tartaros* which was a follow-up to his predecessor Pope Gregory IX's call for a Crusade against the Mongols. As a result of this activity, Dominic of Aragon was sent to woo the Armenians and John of Plano Carpino, an elderly Franciscan, was sent to contact the Mongols. The story of his journey with his companion, Benedict the Pole, through Russia to the camp of the great Khan at Karakoram is an extraordinary tale. They arrived in July 1246 just in time to attend the proclamation of Guyuk Khan as Great Khan. What the Mongols can have thought of these saintly men dressed in their brown habits and bare-footed, neither of whom spoke any oriental language, we do not know; but it is hard to believe that they were greatly impressed by them.

The embassies were not all one way, for about this time St Louis, King of France, was visited by two Mongol envoys, while he was in Cyprus. In return, an embassy under André de Longjumeau in 1249–51 went to the Mongol Queen Regent, then in the Altai region, offering her an alliance. Her reply was crude and to the point : 'Send me large sums of money and place yourselves under my rule, or I will destroy your kingdom.' Undaunted, in 1253 St Louis sent another embassy, this time headed by a certain Franciscan of Flemish extraction, William of Rubruck, whose travels and descriptions of Mongol life and customs make fascinating reading. But nothing came of all these efforts; the distances were too great and the possibilities of effective co-operation too slight for an alliance to have been a practical proposition.

HULAGU AND THE CHRISTIANS

The Mongols were not particularly hostile to Christianity, indeed beyond Shamanism they had no religious feeling or scruples of any kind. They were ruthless in their conquests and followed a policy of deliberate extermination, which resulted in the virtual extinction of the whole populations of towns such as Merv and Nishapur. The Persians say that the backbone of their country was broken by this hideous policy, whose effects are still remembered by Persians today. The thorough destruction of all that the previous centuries had built up and the almost total disruption of trade and everyday life make one marvel that anything survived at all. Hulagu, Genghiz Khan's grandson, became Il Khan of Persia under the suzerainty of the Great Khan and he soon engaged in an aggressive drive towards the West. The particular object of his enmity was Egypt, now under the Mamelukes, who were staunch orthodox Muslims. In 1258, with the help of Georgian troops, he captured Baghdad and perhaps because the Georgians were Christians, the Church there was given favourable treatment. The following year he left Tabriz on a campaign against Egypt; in 1260 Aleppo and Damascus fell, but his hopes were cut short by the Mameluke general, Baybars, who inflicted a decisive defeat on the Mongols at Ayn Jalut in Palestine. Berke, the leader of the Kipchak Turks and Khan of the Golden Horde, had become a Muslim, so from then on the Kipchaks turned towards Egypt and Hulagu was compelled to seek for an alliance with Europe.

In addition to this political reason, he also had personal reasons for favouring Christians since his mother and his chief wife were both Christians. According to the historian Bar Hebraeus, two of the Great Khans had been Christians. He also writes: 'In the year 1265 at the beginning of Lent, Hulagu, King of Kings, left this world . . . and in the summer days Dokhus Khatun, the believing Queen, also died. The Christians of all the world mourned the death of these two great luminaries and protagonists of the Christian religion.' How far we can reconcile our modern ideas of what a Christian should be with Hulagu's conduct it is hard to say. But he was not a mere barbarian, as his subsequent conduct showed, and he may well have been more influenced by the Christian ethic that we can know. At any rate he showed considerable interest in the arts and sciences and built a famous astronomical observatory at Marageh. It was during his reign that the great poet Sa'di of Shiraz lived and wrote.

The Christians were now the favoured group in Iran and the Muslims were a despised majority. Unfortunately, the Christians,

D   49

after many years of oppression, did not use their freedom wisely and antagonised their fellow Persians who were Muslims, by treating them in much the same way that they themselves had been treated for so long. One example of their behaviour will suffice. According to a Muslim historian, Christians openly drank wine during the month of fasting and spilled it on the clothes of Muslims and in their mosques. They also held processions in the streets carrying a cross and made the shop-keepers stand up as it passed, ill-treating those who failed to do so.

The failure of the West to respond to the Mongol embassies and the defeat of Christians on the field of battle began to sow doubts in the minds of the Mongols. Moreover, the subtle influence of the superior Persian culture, which was by this time strongly Muslim, was also gradually making the Il Khans more and more disposed towards Islam. In his efforts to establish a firm government in Iran, Hulagu had destroyed the power of the Ismailis or Assassins, who from their castle fortress of Alamut wielded great power and were virtually a state within a state. In so doing he unwittingly paved the way for a unified Islam in the future, since the Assassins, who reflected the ideals of both the old Persian knights and the suppressed Persian peasantry, were the bitterest enemies of orthodox Islam, and with their defeat the way was clear for the triumph of orthodoxy.

THE EMBASSY OF RABBAN SAUMA

In 1265 Hulagu's son Abaqa succeeded him. He had a Christian wife, daughter of the Byzantine Emperor Michael Palaeologus. Abaqa tried unsuccessfully to establish closer ties with the West and when in 1284 Arghun Khan replaced Ahmad, the first Il Khan to become a Muslim, he too tried to carry on Abaqa's efforts for a *rapprochement* with the West. Arghun himself seems to have favoured Buddhism but he was tolerant towards the Christians. He sent a monk, a certain Rabban Sauma, as his envoy to the Pope and the Kings of France and England. The story of this man is one of the most interesting in all Christian history.

Sauma was born in Pekin about 1250 and was ordained as a monk by George, the Nestorian Metropolitan of China. Seven years later he left his native city to become a hermit. He took with him as a companion another Chinese Christian with the baptismal name of Mark. After some time they left their hermitage to go on a pilgrimage to Jerusalem and the Holy Places. They travelled via Tangut (in Tibet), Kashkhar, Tus and Marageh to Sultanieh the Il Khan capital. Here they met the Patriarch, Denha I, who persuaded them to stay. After two years the Patriarch died and the Chinese monk, Mark, was elected in his place, with the title of Yahballaha III. He remained Patriarch for thirty-six years. In 1286–7 the Il Khan and the Patriarch decided to send Sauma as their envoy to the Pope in Rome and to the Kings of England and France. Sauma wrote a full account of his journey in Persian, of which a Syriac version has come down to us. After visiting Byzantium he arrived in Rome, where he was hospitably received and celebrated the Eucharist according to his own rite in the presence of the Pope and his cardinals, and in turn received communion from the hands of the Pope himself. Sauma wisely avoided entering into any doctrinal discussions with his hosts. Next he went on to France where he was entertained by King Philip the Fair; he then proceeded to Bordeaux where he met Edward I of England. King Edward tended to take Rabban Sauma's embassy more seriously since, while on the Crusade in Palestine in 1271, he had sent two envoys, Reginald Russel and John Parker, to the Il Khan Abaqa in order to make arrangements for a joint campaign against the Egyptians; but nothing had come of it – six years later Abaqa sent envoys to apologise for his failure to send help!

While Sauma was in France a new Pope had been elected to take the place of Honorius IV who had died. The new Pope, Nicholas IV, had been a Franciscan missionary in Constantinople and elsewhere and understood the importance of supporting the Christians in the East. He gave Rabban Sauma a letter confirming Yahballaha's title as 'Patriarch over all the Orientals', and sent a letter of condolence to Abaqa's widow. Arghun was very pleased with the results of Sauma's mission and christened his son Nicholas in honour of the Pope, and promised that he himself would be baptised in Jerusalem when it was won back from the Saracens. One cannot help discerning in this offer a deliberate policy of delay, waiting to see which side would emerge victorious in the struggle then in progress. Unfortunately, the West was preoccupied with quarrels and struggles of its own and could spare neither time nor attention for the affairs of far-off Persia. Only Edward I endeavoured to bring about an effective partnership between the Il Khans and the West. But the moment never came.

The final and decisive blow to the prospects of the Persian Church came when Ghazan Khan (1295–1304), realising that he could not rule his Muslim subjects (who were in a large majority) without their co-operation and goodwill, was persuaded by a Persian amir named Nauruz to become a Muslim. This he did in June 1295, when he and all his army were in their summer camp in the Lar valley in the mountains north of Tehran. This was even before he became Il Khan – which took place after his rival was slain on 5 October 1295. His successor, Oljaitu, although nominally a Muslim continued to exchange ambassadors with Europe. But in 1323 the last of the Il Khans, Abu Said, signed a treaty of friendship with the Egyptians, and the solidarity of the Islamic world was finally evident to all.

Under such circumstances the Church was bound to suffer. The Patriarchs, as important religious leaders, were tolerated and even respected by the Muslim rulers, but Christianity in Persia as a whole entered into a period of rapid decline. Numerous churches were closed, episcopal sees fell vacant and new bishops were not appointed. Christians in Persia became a small and insignificant minority of little importance in the political and diplomatic life of the country.

THE FIRST DOMINICAN MISSIONARIES

From late in the thirteenth century, the north of Persia and the neighbouring vassal states of Georgia and Armenia had been the field of Roman Catholic missionary endeavour. The work was carried on by members of the Franciscan and Dominican orders and came under the control of the vast Archdiocese of Khanbalik or Pekin in China, instituted in 1309, which was administered by the Franciscans. In 1306 John of Monte Corvino, later to become first Archbishop of Khanbalik, was writing letters to the Vicar-General of the Preachers in the Province of Persia. Persia was the most important mission field of the Dominican order both in extent and in duration (it continued until the eighteenth century). By about 1300 there were three centres of work: Tabriz, Dehikerkan and Maragheh. Soon after this, a new impulse was given to the mission by the arrival of some of the *Frères Pérégrinants* (the missionary branch of the Dominican order). They reopened the post at Sivas and decided to start up a new post at Sultanieh, which in 1313 became the capital and residence of Oljaitu. In 1314 Franco de Pérouse founded a convent there and in 1318 a Papal Bull was issued creating a new Archdiocese of Sultanieh, separated from the Archdiocese of Pekin. Franco de Pérouse was the first Archbishop. This was done at the instigation of a former Dominican missionary in Persia, Guillaume Adam, who was then in France and wrote a tract with the unfortunate title of *De Modo Saracenos Extirpandi*. He later became Archbishop of Sultanieh. With the Archbishop, six suffragans were also appointed but without specifying where their sees were to be. The new Archdiocese was to include the whole of the Persian Empire ruled by the Mongols, except the territories west of Mount Ararat, Transoxiana and the whole of India. But in all this vast area the Archbishop was hard put to find six locations where there were Dominicans at work and where there was the nucleus of a Christian congregation. Three bishops were appointed to places outside the area designated by the Papal Bull; Guillaume Adam went to Izmir, Bernard de Plaisance to Sivas, and Bernard Moreti to Sebastopol. The three sees inside the designated area were the old posts of Tabriz, where Father Barthélemy Abaglati was the first bishop, and Dehikerkan to which Gérard Calvet was appointed; Maragheh, where the Nestorian Catholicos had his seat, was the see of the famous Barthélemy of Bologna. By 1328 this same Barthélemy was the only remaining Latin bishop in Persia; he left Persia in this year and died in 1333. Before he left he inaugurated the work which gave rise to the foundation of the famous Uniate Order of Armenian Monks, the Brothers of St Gregory the Illuminator (*Fratres Unitores*). For many years after this, the Roman missionaries concentrated their activities amongst the Christian communities of Armenia and Georgia, with work centred on Nakhchivan in Armenia. Individual monks remained in Persia proper for a while but natural disasters took their toll, such as the plague in 1348 which killed all the missionaries. Political upheavals were also taking place; after the death in 1335 of the last member of the Il Khan dynasty a period of anarchy supervened, and for a time rival dynasties ruled in the north and the south.

'THE SCOURGE OF GOD'

An end was put to confusion and very much else besides in 1369 when the dreaded Mongol leader Timur-e-Lang appeared on the scene. Timur the Lame was a descendant of Genghiz Khan whose exploits he was to emulate and exceed. He is also known to us as Tamburlane; he whom Marlowe rightly called, 'the scourge of God and terror of the world'. Timur unleashed a new reign of terror in Iran. The great Czech scholar, Jan Rypka, states categorically that 'in bestial cruelty Timur even managed to outdo the Mongols of unhappy memory'.

No estimate can be made of the number of people killed in Timur's campaigns, but hundreds of thousands died and among them were many Christians. This time the whole of Iran was devastated. Once again, much of what had been precariously built up during the Il Khan period was swept away and the Christian Church ceased to function as an organised body. The savagery dealt it a mortal blow from which it never fully recovered and it disappears from the scene of Iranian history as an organisation exerting any influence on the affairs of the country (see pp. 78–79).

But it was not only the decimation of its members by Timur that destroyed the Church; this was only the consummation of a process of decay which had been going on for 100 years or more. Ultimately the failure of the Church was due to internal weaknesses. It had not grown intellectually; indeed, Professor Burkitt described it as 'intellectually timid'. It also relied heavily on monasticism and presented asceticism and retreat from the world as the normal Christian way of life. It also failed in other ways to appeal to the mass of the people: its theology was too complicated and, as far as we know, it insisted on using Syriac for its language of worship. In addition to all this, the simplicity of Islam and its identification in the national mind with being a Persian, all contributed to the failure of Christianity at this time. But although Islam triumphed because of its greater appeal, Christianity has, nevertheless, been a continuing strand in the inner life of Iran and runs like a hidden stream through much of its poetry and its philosophy. Professor A. J. Arberry, enlarging on a line of Hafez, has interpreted it thus:

> And if the Holy Ghost descend
> In grace and power infinite
> His comfort in these days to lend
> To them that humbly wait on it,
> Theirs too the wondrous works can be
> That Jesus wrought in Galilee.

Part Two

THE ROMAN CATHOLIC ERA

Chapter Seven

THE ROMAN CATHOLIC MISSIONARY EFFORT

EARLY HISTORY

The aftermath of Timur-e-Lang's incredible fury left Iran in a state of extreme exhaustion and despair, without any centralised government or even a potentially powerful leader in sight. For some years, rival Turkoman tribes in the north fought under the banners of The Black Sheep and The White Sheep. Eventually Uzun Hasan (Hasan the Tall), leader of The White Sheep, prevailed and became overlord, with some sort of control over most of Persia.

Uzun Hasan, who reigned from 1453 to 1478, had family links with Byzantium, for his great-grandmother had been a Christian. In 1458 David, the last Comnene Emperor of Trebizond, gave his niece, Kyra Katerina (who is usually known by her Greek title of Despina, that is Signora), to Hasan in marriage. In 1461 her father's kingdom, the last Christian enclave in Turkey, fell to the Ottoman attacks.

The rise of Turkish power and its continued aggressive forays, both eastwards into Persia and westwards into Europe, made an alliance between the two a logical proposition. This proposition, that both Persia and Europe were threatened by Ottoman aggression, remained true for the two and a half centuries that followed the fall of Constantinople in 1453. But logic was not enough to bring the two parties together. Throughout the period we read of the abortive efforts of the two sides to come together and work in a meaningful way for the defeat of their common enemy. One such effort was made in 1463–5 when there was an exchange of embassies between Uzun Hasan and the Republic of Venice. In 1471 Querini (the first Venetian Ambassador) was replaced by Despina's nephew, Catarino Zeno, but no constructive proposals were forthcoming from either side. Eventually, as we shall see, Persia, after repeated failures on the part of the European powers to do anything constructive, opted

57

for the lesser evil of patching up some sort of friendship with the Ottomans who at least had the doubtful virtue of proximity.

THE EMERGENCE OF THE SAFAVIS

For some twenty years after Uzun Hasan's death a new period of anarchy prevailed in Iran. Eventually, after some difficult campaigning, a new leader emerged who became a founder of the Safavi dynasty; he was Ismail, the descendant of a certain Sheikh Saif-ud-din Ishaq, a Sufi religious leader, who lived at Ardebil in north-western Persia. Sheikh Saif-ud-din was a Sunni, but his descendants joined the Shia sect, thus distinguishing themselves from the Ottoman Turks who were fanatical Sunnis. The Sheikh's descendants gradually became the leaders of a federation of local tribes who united to resist encroachments from outside, notably from the Turks.

Shah Ismail had a double claim to Persian loyalty, for he was not only the descendant of a great religious leader, but he was also the grandson of Uzun Hasan. He made good use of both these facts. It is noteworthy that the appeal of the Safavi dynasty lay in the revival of the ancient, pre-Islamic (Persian) idea of loyalty to the monarch, reinforced by religious belief in the sacred nature of the Shah. Ismail was seen to be a reincarnation of Ali, the founding father of the Shia sect, and he proclaimed in his poetry that *sijdeh* was due to him; the word he employed is normally used for prostration before God. He gathered round himself a group, known as the Shahsevan (friends of the King), to whom he gave esoteric teaching and who were fanatically loyal to him.

This union of religious and political power in the person of the Shah was encouraged, at least implicitly, by all the subsequent members of the dynasty. It would account for the care with which Karim Khan Zand, after the fall of the dynasty, refrained from pronouncing himself Shah and instead adopted the title of *Vakil* or Regent. It would also account for the acquiescence of the Persian people when confronted with the extortionate cruelty of their Shahs, and also for the extreme difficulty of making any impression on their religious beliefs.

In 1511 a great Shia rebellion broke out at Tekke in Turkey and the Sultan Selim decided to extirpate all the heretics in his dominions. 40,000 were killed, and this slaughter brought a protest from Shah Ismail, which prompted Selim to attack Persia. He did so with some success, taking Tabriz and the province of Kurdistan and Diabekr. Ismail died in 1524 and was succeeded by his son, Tahmasp. The fortunes of war fluctuated, but the tide was gradually turning in favour of the Persians. In 1535 the Persians defeated the Turks near Lake Van; in 1548 with the help of Portuguese cannon and gunners they again defeated them on the banks of the Euphrates. Finally, in 1553, the Turkish Sultan Suleiman in person, at the head of an enormous army, attacked Persia and was defeated.

In 1507, the Portuguese, under the great Albuquerque, took possession of the island of Hormoz in the Persian Gulf and rapidly turned it into an immensely rich trading centre with a mixed population of Arabs, Jews and Persians and representatives of the trading interests of many nations. From about 1575 a number of members of the Portuguese order of Augustinian Hermits came to Hormoz to minister to the many Catholics there. In 1559 the first English merchants reached Persia via Russia and their reports may be read in Hakluyt's *Collection of Voyages*.

From now on Persia was to become the stamping ground of almost every European country seeking political and commercial concessions, all deeply suspicious of the others and carrying on all sorts of intrigues in order to get the upper hand. In 1562 Anthony Jenkinson arrived in Qazvin as the commercial envoy of Queen Elizabeth of England. In 1571, after the battle of Lepanto, Pope Pius V wrote to Tahmasp urging continued resistance to the Turks, and in 1579 Pope Gregory drew up draft instructions for a possible envoy to Persia, but the approach was dilatory and unrealistic. In 1582 the Portuguese Viceroy of India, on the instructions of King Philip, sent Father Simon Morales, the Prior of the Augustinian Convent on Hormoz, who could speak Persian, as his envoy to Shah Khodabandeh. Father Simon was well received at the Persian court and was asked to teach the Crown Prince, Hamzeh Mirza, mathematics and the use of the spheres. Hamzeh was an attractive young man and showed some interest in Christianity and Father Simon seems to have had hopes that he might be converted. But like all future missionary ambassadors he found his position invidious. He would have endorsed the words of another such, who wrote, 'nous sommes chargés des choses de nostre ambassade fort impertinentes et pénibles pour nos intentions'.

Another effort was made in 1584 when Pope Gregory XIII sent a certain Venetian nobleman Giambattista Vecchietti to the East with the twofold intention of conciliating the Coptic Patriarch of Alexandria and of offering an alliance to the Shah of Persia in his struggle against the Turks. Vecchietti came to the court of the Shah at Tabriz and was cordially received, but nothing came of his diplomatic efforts.

During his travels in Persia he collected a number of manuscripts of the Bible, written in Judaeo-Persian. He did not pursue his diplomatic career but he did return to Persia again in 1601 in search of more Biblical manuscripts. Many of the manuscripts which he collected eventually found their way into the Vatican and other important libraries. They include an early and important Judaeo-Persian Pentateuch and various versions of the Psalms and the Prophetic Books, which Vecchietti's zeal certainly saved from destruction. But he was not only interested in collecting these manuscripts but also in transliterating them into the Persian script and thus providing the Persians with the Old Testament – at least in Persian. This he began to do with the help of a Persian Christian, Shams-ud-Din Khandji.

In 1604 he visited India, where his fame had preceded him, and the Mogul Emperor Akbar expressed a desire to meet him, which he did, receiving him with great interest. While in India Vecchietti continued with his transliteration, helped by the native Christians. He also made friends with the Jesuit missionaries, especially with Jerome Xavier. On leaving India (where he had been joined by his brother) he once again travelled through Persia. During the sea voyage home to Italy he was captured by pirates, who held him prisoner for a short time, so that he did not reach Rome until 1608. His efforts to interest the authorities in his Persian manuscripts were unsuccessful and he died neglected and in poverty in 1619.

Shah Khodabandeh's last days were typically tragic. His first son, Hamzeh Mirza, died at the end of 1586. His second son, Abbas, blinded and imprisoned his father and took complete control in 1587–8 – in October 1588 he officially became King.

Shah Abbas's early years were spent warding off hostile attacks from the east and from the west. His successes were frequent enough to make Pope Clement VIII think it worth while to write suggesting an alliance. But once again the negotiations came to nothing. In 1598 the site of the capital was moved from Qazvin in the north to Isfahan in the centre of the country, where it was less accessible to Turkish attacks. The following year two Englishmen, Robert and Anthony Sherley, arrived in Isfahan. Anthony, the more brash and enterprising of the two, soon persuaded the Shah to send him to Europe as his Ambassador. He was by no means a reliable envoy and there seems little doubt that he seriously misrepresented the situation in Persia and the intentions of the Shah, to the European courts which he visited.

Sherley, his Persian colleague and their retinue arrived in Rome in July 1599. While they were there his cook and two more of his retinue announced their conversion to Christianity. In Spain, where they went next, three of his secretaries, one of whom was his own nephew, also became Christians. One of these three, Ulug Beg, son of Sultan Ali Beg, who had been killed fighting the Turks at Tabriz, became famous as the Don Juan of Persia. He was baptised in the palace chapel at Valladolid, the Queen of Spain being his sponsor. He subsequently wrote and published a travel diary and history of Persia. As a result of these occurrences the Pope was led to believe that Shah Abbas was well disposed towards Christianity and would welcome Christian missionaries and might even become a Christian himself. Nothing in fact could have been farther from the truth. The character of this great man is exceedingly difficult to judge at this distance of time, but he seems to have been one of those typically Persian figures who appear on the stage of Persian history from time to time. They seem rather larger than life and appear at times when the country's fortunes are at a very low ebb. By force of personality and ruthless determination, they rescue the country from its troubles and put it firmly on its feet again and impose some order on the naturally individualistic Persians. Shah Abbas was an autocrat; he once asked a European Ambassador whether the Kings of Europe were as autocratic as he was. On being told that they were not, he replied: 'well, the difference is that they have men to rule, whereas I have untamed animals'. Everything and everyone had to be subordinated to the will of the King. One sad result which is seen in the life of Shah Abbas and also in the life of others of his ilk, is that as he grew older he developed a pathological suspicion of everyone, especially his relatives, and he eventually succumbed to increasing bouts of megalomania which resulted in mounting tyranny and innumerable acts of extreme cruelty and viciousness.

SHAH ABBAS: POTENTIAL CONVERT OR
POLITICAL ALLY?

In 1601 two more Portuguese envoys (also Augustinians) were sent
with instructions to put religious matters first and to work for the
conversion of the Shah. The two men chosen were singularly unsuitable and having quarrelled with each other for the whole of their
journey out, they behaved so badly at court that they became
figures of fun and brought a lot of ridicule on the Christian cause.
However, in 1603–4 two real missionaries from Goa arrived. But
they were Portuguese envoys first and missionaries second. Their
mission had no official backing from the Pope and as the author of
The Chronicle of the Carmelites, writes of them: they 'were Portuguese and *not there as missionaries of their order* [author's italics]
but purely as diplomatists to push the interests of the authorities
of Hormoz and Goa.' But whatever the mixture of their motives,
they were well received and given a house in Isfahan where they
settled down and founded a convent. So from the very first, religion
and politics were inextricably mixed up and to this day many
Persians cannot believe that missionaries are not the employees of
their government, sent to act on their behalf.

During the early years of the reign of Shah Abbas, Jesuits were
at work at the Mogul court in India. The language of the court
was Persian and one of the missionaries, Father Jerome Xavier,
nephew of St Francis Xavier, translated a number of works into
Persian. In 1602 he wrote a life of Christ called *Dastane Massih*,
which gained a certain notoriety because it included legendary
matter not found in the Gospels. In 1638 it was printed in Leiden
with a Latin translation by a Dutch Protestant orientalist, Ludovic
de Dieu, to show how corrupt Catholic teaching was.

Xavier also wrote an apologetic work called *A'ina-i Haqq Nama*
or *The Truth Revealing Mirror* which, according to a contemporary
writer, was sent by the Great Mogul to the Shah of Persia. At any
rate it was well known in court circles at the time of Shah Abbas
and provoked various responses. Notable among the replies to this
work was one by a Persian, Ahmad ben Zain ul Abedin, who had
been shown the *A'ina-i Haqq Nama* by the Carmelite Fathers. His
reply was so powerful that the Carmelites felt it could not be left
unanswered and it was sent to Rome where a Franciscan scholar,
Father Philip Guadagnoli, wrote an answer which was published in

Rome in 1631 under the title *Apologia pro Christiana Religione*. It was said, but with what truth it is hard to say, that Father Philip's book so impressed Ahmad that he became a Christian. At any rate the controversy seems to have been conducted in an unusually friendly and courteous manner on both sides.

At the turn of the century, Turkish power was on the wane and the effects of Shah Abbas's ruthless activities were beginning to show. In 1604 he carried out the first of his compulsory mass movements of populations, by forcing the inhabitants of Christian Armenia, which lay on the north-west frontier of Iran, to leave their country and to settle in various parts of Persia. The exact numbers displaced in this way are not really known, but it would seem that the following figures are quite reliable. According to Tavernier, Du Mans and Chardin, those transferred to the northern provinces of Gilan and Mazanderan numbered about 20,000–30,000 families; the Armenian historian, Arakel of Tabriz, however, gives 10,000 families as his estimate. They were settled in or around the newly-founded capital of Farahabad, and their descendants are to be found today in the Armenian colony of Tabriz. Those transferred to the southern provinces numbered about 12,000 families or 75,000 souls. They were settled on the south bank of the river Zayandehrud near Isfahan, where they built a township which they called New Julfa. Others were settled in the surrounding countryside, where predominantly Armenian villages are still to be found to this day.

Many of the Armenians who settled in New Julfa were skilled craftsmen and were used by Shah Abbas in the many public works which he initiated for the embellishment of his new capital. The incorporation of a large body of Christians into the very heartland of Persia and their continuing presence in the country was to have a very considerable effect on the future of Persia. From now on they were always confronted with a body of devoted Christians, who in spite of many attempts to induce them to abandon their faith and adopt Islam very rarely did so.

The great Armenian historian, Pasdermadjian, writes of the Armenian role in world history as follows:

As Charles Peguy has remarked: 'A nation is not only a state and a frontier, it is above all a mission.' In the case of Armenia, this mission was to serve as intermediary and interpreter between East and West. Armenia played that part in antiquity between Rome and Parthia and pursued it in the Middle Ages between

Byzantium and the Arab Empire and in modern times between Europe and the Muslim East.

One of the early envoys sent by Uzun Hasan to Venice was an Armenian and subsequently numerous Armenians have acted as Persian Ambassadors on various occasions, right up to the twentieth century.

It was naturally a bitter blow to the Armenian community that so much of the Roman Catholic effort should have been directed towards persuading them to leave their ancient Church to which they were so fiercely attached and to try by various means to induce them to join the Church of Rome. On more than one occasion they accused the missionaries of wanting to make them 'Portuguese' or *Farangis* of some kind, and their loyalty to Persia and to their own form of Christianity was quite misunderstood by the missionaries. The Armenians of New Julfa desired to retain at all costs whatever pertained to their nationhood, since they were the only Armenian community in Persia which can be said to have really taken root and flourished at this time.

OBSTACLES TO MISSIONARY SUCCESS

The main outlines of the conditions under which missionary work was to be carried out for the next 150 years were soon laid down; and once laid down they seemed to change very little. First, the missionaries had to contend with their dual role as advocates of an alien religion, on the one hand, and as diplomats of a foreign power on the other. Secondly, partly through their own choice and partly against their will, much of their time was taken up with sterile controversies with the Armenian Church. Thirdly, the political influence of the European powers and the general prosperity and stability of the country declined steadily throughout this period. For most of the time there was an actual state of war and when there was peace it was uneasy and of short duration.

The dissensions within the Christian body were perhaps ultimately the most serious disincentives to the spread of the Christian religion. For not only was there the running warfare between the Roman Catholics and the Armenians, which scarcely ever let up, but there were also frequent clashes between the different Orders representing different European countries. Further clashes occurred when Protestant countries like England and Holland sent commercial representatives to Persia, as exemplified by the occasion when the Dutch

Factor, a Protestant, tried to get all the Roman Catholic missions expelled from the country. Small wonder that Père Bernard de Sainte Thérèse wrote in a letter (1641): 'J'advoue que les Chrestiens de ce pays ici me font incomparablement plus de peine que les infidelles.' He had been attacked because he refused to sanction the marriage of a Dutch Protestant with an Arab Catholic girl.

THE COMING OF THE CARMELITES

On 6 July 1604 the Papal Mission of the Discalced (Barefooted) Carmelites left Rome for Persia. Owing to the state of virtual civil war at the time in Russia, they were a long time reaching their destination, not arriving in Isfahan until late in 1607. For the next 150 years the Carmelites were to be the most devoted and persevering Christian missionaries in Persia. They can count among their number many devoted and deeply spiritual men who by their charity, poverty and sincerity made a lasting impression on all who met them. But from the point of view of gaining diplomatic advantages they had arrived too late. Very soon after their arrival the leader of the mission, Father Paul Simon, wrote to the Pope: 'All I can inform your Holiness is that the King of Persia is very powerful and no longer has need of Christian princes to help him.' Nevertheless, the Carmelites were accepted and given a house to live in. They were received by the Shah in January 1608. They gave him the presents they had brought with them; a cross made of gold and Bohemian crystal, a book of Old Testament miniatures and a small barrel of vodka, from the emperor of Russia; it appears that the last-named gift was the most acceptable.

Father Paul Simon soon returned to Rome to report to the Pope on the situation and prospects of the new mission. His long written report has survived and many of the suggestions in it have a curiously modern ring. 'It is unnecessary', he wrote, 'that missionaries should be well versed in theology (though that can do no harm) . . . what is more requisite is personal holiness and to set a good example. The third requisite is that the labourers who go out there should have great disdain for wealth and accept nothing.' A year's further experience enabled Father John Thaddeus, who stayed with the mission, to write: 'As to the character of the King, at heart he is a Muslim and all he has done in the past has been feigned.' Father John, a saintly man and a good linguist, soon became intimate with

E
65

the Shah, who even borrowed his spectacles on occasion. He trusted
him so much that in 1611 he sent him as his Ambassador to the
Czar of Russia, the King of Poland and the Pope. The mission was
never accomplished as Father John was arrested at Astrakhan in
Russia on suspicion of being a Persian spy. He was thrown into
prison and tortured; only the strenuous intervention of Shah Abbas
secured his release early in 1614, whereupon he returned to the
comparative security of Isfahan.

But however much Father John found himself willy-nilly involved
in politics, he was at heart a true missionary. He made many very
sensible and forward-looking suggestions, which if they had been
implemented might have hastened the building up of an indigenous
Church. But, alas, they were all turned down by the authorities
in Rome. He suggested that the Missal might be translated into
Persian or Turkish (the language of the court) and permission should
be given to celebrate the Mass in these languages. He also wrote
that: 'the sort of men this Shah would be glad to have sent to him
are: clockmakers, musicians, painters, those who would be talented
enough to construct fountains and suchlike things; but it is essential
that they should have a firm belief in the faith, because otherwise
there is a great risk in these countries . . . that they might be persuaded by acts and words to abandon it.' But the day of industrial
missionaries was still in the future. He also suggested that a college
be founded in Isfahan for Armenian, Georgian, Circassian and
Persian boys, who (he says) may be purchased for small sums from
the many offered for sale. The sale of children frequently crops up
in the missionaries' letters of this time; in order to meet the extortionate demands of the Shah and his ministers parents frequently
had to resort to this desperate expedient. But no school was built
and Father John's vision of a missionary school was not realised for
another 200 years or more. In the meantime Father John occupied
his time by preaching to the villagers around Isfahan and ministering
to any Christians who needed his help.

In 1614, Shah Abbas continued his policy of creating a neutral
and deserted zone around the borders of his country by forcibly
removing between 50,000 and 60,000 families, all Christians, from
the province of Kakheti in eastern Georgia. Georgia like Armenia
was one of those small buffer states whose overlordship was constantly being disputed by Persians, Turks and local princes. These
hapless families were settled in villages around Isfahan and Shiraz.

Among those captured and brought to Persia was King Louarsab. The Khan of Shiraz endeavoured to make him accept Islam, but he refused to do so and was strangled. Ten years later the famous Georgian martyr, Queen Ketevan, was also to die in Shiraz after atrocious tortures, for refusing to deny her faith.

About this time a strange figure turned up in Isfahan: George Strachan of Mearns, a Catholic exile from Scotland, who after becoming the physician to a beduin sheikh and contracting some sort of a marriage with a close relative of his master, thought it politic to leave his employment. He then turned up in Isfahan as an employee of the East India Company. Owing to the machinations of a disgruntled and neurotic colleague, Strachan was dismissed. However, he was taken in by the Carmelites whose kindness he repaid by giving them Arabic lessons. He became friendly with Pietro della Valle and eventually disappears from history somewhere between Persia and India. He made a valuable collection of oriental manuscripts which are now in the Vatican and other libraries.

In 1620 an incident took place, which those who know Persia will surely recognise as typical. It was the custom of the Armenians at Epiphanytide to conduct a very solemn and gorgeous ceremony of Blessing the Waters of the Zayandehrud River in Isfahan. Shah Abbas often used to attend this ceremony; he was not exactly an easy or a tactful guest, but he was the Shah and his presence was considered an honour. Gorgeous processions from all the Churches in Julfa converged on the river, followed by most of the Catholic missionaries and the King and his courtiers. This year Shah Abbas took over the proceedings, directing the unfortunate Armenian clergy where to stand and what to do. When the ceremony was over the King accompanied them back to Julfa and spent most of the day in religious discussions with them. In the evening he asked to see some of their relics, which were reluctantly shown to him. At first he treated them with respect, kissing them and telling those who stood round to behave reverently before such holy objects. Among the most sacred of the relics was a bone of Saint Ripsima; the Shah took it into his head to give some of it to Father John Thaddeus, so he calmly took the relic and broke off a piece, wrapped it in paper and gave it to the embarrassed Father John.

In 1621 the East India Company's factor, Edward Monnox, and his chaplain were presented to the Shah. The Carmelite Visitor-General was also present at the audience and the Shah had some fun hearing them discuss the differences between Catholic and Protestant; the poor Anglican chaplain seems to have got the worst of the argument. The first contact with the English, apart from the occasional visits of merchants via Russia and the egregious Sherley brothers, had taken place in 1615 when the East India Company sent Richard Steele and John Crowther to solicit the Shah's permission for the East India Company's vessels to visit Persian ports. With the help of Robert Sherley this permission and certain other commercial favours were granted and the Company soon became an important factor in the commercial and political life of the country. The Dutch were soon to follow them and thus the Protestant influence was established.

1621 was a difficult year for the missionaries but worse was to come. The Armenians were severely persecuted and many thousands were compelled to renounce their faith or die. In the autumn, tension grew over the future of Hormoz Island and the Augustinians and other Catholic missionaries were under suspicion. In the spring of 1622 the Persians captured the outer city and with British help took the castle and became masters of the whole island. The Portuguese left for Muscat or India and the whole of the missionary work there, with its churches and hospices, was abandoned – only the bell from the Carmelite church was saved and sent to Shiraz.

It was during these troubled times that five Persian martyrs met their death. The Carmelites' gardener, Chassader, had become a Christian and with him, his brother-in-law, Elie, and three others. In 1621 Chassader and Elie were sent with letters to the Carmelites on Hormoz Island warning them of danger. As they passed through Shiraz they were recognised by an Englishman, who suspected that they might be spies. He had them arrested and handed over to the Khan, who put them in prison and took their letters. They freely admitted to being Christians. After several days of starvation they still refused to recant, so Chassader was publicly disembowelled and the unfortunate Elie was wrapped in a donkey's skin, impaled on a stake and left to die. The letters they carried giving the names of the other Christians were sent to the Shah. On being summoned to the Shah's camp outside Isfahan, the men at first denied their faith but later publicly acknowledged it and were stoned to death and their bodies burnt.

Life was indeed hard for Christians at that time but Father John Thaddeus could write: 'Although Hormoz has been taken by the

Muhammadans as a chastisement and punishment of the Christians and we are close pressed on all sides and deprived of all spiritual and financial assistance, courage does not fail us on that account. We now begin to be disciples of Christ.' 1623 was a very bad year for them; anyone showing an interest in Christianity was persecuted. New extortionate demands were made upon the Armenians, for several months the Carmelite Fathers were confined to the convent and all their outside work was stopped; they were no longer the confidants of the Shah and money was very short indeed. Nevertheless, it was in this year that in faith they ventured to buy a house in Shiraz on the road to Lar where they remained until 1656. They were welcomed there by the common people who used to visit the church for *ziarat*, or pilgrimage, until they were forbidden to do so by the authorities. In 1626–7 the Augustinian mission was finally banished from Isfahan and nearly 100 years of Portuguese influence was at an end.

In 1628 the representatives of yet another European power appeared on the scene. This time it was France, who decided to send a group of missionary diplomats of the Capuchin order of Friars Minor. The plan seems to have originated in the fertile mind of Père Joseph, the *éminence grise* of Cardinal Richelieu. Two of the three delegates, Père Pacifique de Provins and Père Gabriel de Chinon have left valuable accounts of their time in Persia. For the rest of the century this order lived and worked in Persia where they were everywhere recognised as envoys of the King of France. In 1628 a printing press and type-founding materials were at last sent to Persia, having been first asked for in 1619 by Father John Thaddeus, but there is no evidence remaining that they were ever put into use. Later we read that Father Bernard de Sainte Thérèse also brought printing materials. But since Islam is fundamentally opposed to printing, no use seems to have been made of them. A much more successful effort was that of the Armenian church at Julfa which set up a press at this time; the first of its kind in the Middle East.

Shortly before he died in 1629 Shah Abbas issued the edict which did more than any other single act to blight the chances of Christians in Persia. The edict said that any Christian who became a Muslim could claim all the property of his relations for seven generations back (later reduced to four). By 1654 it was estimated that at least 50,000 Christians had apostasised in order to retain their patrimony – few of them, however, were from the Armenian community.

In 1632 the veteran John Thaddeus went to Rome to be consecrated Bishop of Isfahan. His diocese covered the whole of Persia, all Georgia and Greater and Lesser Armenia, with the exception of the province of Nakhchivan which had its own bishop of the Dominican order. Very sadly for the future of the mission and the Christian cause, Bishop John never returned to his diocese. On a journey to collect recruits in his native Spain his mule ran away with him on a mountain track and he was killed.

The new Shah Safi, grandson of Shah Abbas, was less cruel than his predecessor and seems to have been genuinely inclined to be well disposed towards the Christians. Contemporary records describe him as clement and pleasant in all his dealings, and say that no Christians were persecuted during his reign. But external conditions grew worse; the Turks were attacking again and in 1630 took Hamadan, and the threat of their proceeding to invest Isfahan seemed so serious that four of the seven religious then in Isfahan left for Basra. The scare passed, however, and the Fathers returned and, with a legacy from a wealthy Genoese merchant, began to build a church in Isfahan which was completed in 1638. It was a fine building with four side chapels and a bell-tower with two bells which were rung throughout the day and the night at the times of the Office. Its exact site is unknown.

Onu the death of Bishop John the appointment of his successor was in the hands of the French, since the endowment for the Bishop of Isfahan came from the legacy of a Madame Ricouart which stipulated that all future Bishops of Isfahan must be of French nationality. On the recommendation of Queen Anne of Austria, Father Bernard de Sainte Thérèse, a French Carmelite, was appointed and he eventually arrived in Isfahan in 1640. He was a scholarly man and the inventory of the books, which he left on his death in the house he had bought, proves that he was also a good linguist. But he was old and after building a fine residence and cathedral church in the Sheikh Sava'n district of Isfahan and after embarrassing the poor Carmelite Fathers by the size of his entourage, he returned to Paris and spent the rest of his long life there, refusing to return to his see. The Fathers kept up services in the cathedral until 1653 when lack of funds forced them to abandon it.

The weather, as time passed, completed its destruction and nothing of it remains today.

In 1649 one of the most faithful and energetic of the Carmelite Fathers, Father Dimas, paid a visit to the areas around Shiraz and Persepolis where the unfortunate Georgians had been settled. He visited, amongst other places, Ramgird, north-west of Persepolis and Durudzan, then known as Cherkessabad from the many Circassians living there. He found that many of the Christians, left without pastoral care of any kind, had succumbed to the pressures of their environment and become Muslims, but at that time they had not forgotten their faith and many wished to return to it. But not sufficient was done to encourage them and they were so neglected over the succeeding centuries that today no trace of them remains. Indeed, the experience of an English missionary in the 1930s might be the last sign of this once Christian community. On visiting villages round Shiraz with a medical team, she found a village family where the mother made the sign of the cross over the bread before distributing it. She did not know why she did so, but said that it was just their custom; in all other respects she was a Muslim.

Shah Safi died in 1642 and was succeeded by Shah Abbas II, a nine-year-old boy. During his reign European diplomatic influence and activity decreased, whereas the co-operation between the Persians and the Turks began to increase; they were inclined to forget their doctrinal feuds and to make common cause against the Christians. The new Shah's policy reflected this change of outlook and the faithful Carmelites had to carry on under increasing disabilities. In 1653 the first of the Jesuit missionaries arrived, Father Aimé Chezaud, who was followed in 1655 by Father François Rigordi. The Jesuits settled in Julfa, where some years previously the Sacred Congregation had authorised the establishment of a special mission. The influx of 'Frank' missionaries was strongly resented by the Armenians who in 1654 tried unsuccessfully to have all foreign missionaries expelled by the Shah. However, their anger was so great that many of the Fathers thought it wiser to retire from Julfa for a time.

The Carmelites, ever on the outlook for new fields of service, sent Father Dionysius of the Crown of Thorns in 1652 on an adventurous visit to the Nestorians round Lake Urmiah. He found 40,000 families living there in great poverty and ignorance. He contacted the Patriarch and took a letter from him to the Pope.

Itinerant evangelism still continued and the baptism of children *in articulo mortis* was carried on with great zeal. But the times were unpropitious for long-term planning and the missionaries received scant visible reward for their long years of devoted and patient work.

In 1656 the Capuchins founded a small house in Tabriz. While in Isfahan one of their number, Father Raphael du Mans, became famous as a mathematician and scientist. He spent over fifty years in Persia, dying in 1696 at the age of 83. His book, *Estat de la Perse en 1660*, provides a valuable historical account of the country as he knew it. In 1661 a Benedictine Monsignor Placid du Chemin was appointed Bishop of Neo-Caesarea with future succession to the see of Babylon or Isfahan when the absentee Bishop Bernard eventually died, but Monsignor Placid du Chemin too never visited his diocese.

GROWING ANARCHY

On the death of Shah Abbas II in 1666 the country slipped deeper and deeper into anarchy and lawlessness. His successor, Suleiman, was a drunkard and a womaniser. In 1672 one of the missionaries reported that: 'The King is always busy drinking, there is neither anyone who governs nor is there any order – everything makes for the oppression of Christians.' Lawlessness increased and the unsubdued tribespeople threatened the safety of travellers. Children called out in the streets after the missionaries 'Dog, become a Muslim' or 'Cursed be the *Farangis*'. By 1678 the extortionate demands and persecution of all the minorities reached a peak. Many thousands of Jews were murdered and the Armenians, who had already been robbed of almost everything they possessed, were yet again subjected to the most extravagant demands, with the threat of mass extermination if they refused to pay up. Children were sold openly for a few *sols* and many young girls were abducted for the Shah's harem. In 1683, after the Blessing of the Waters ceremony, twenty-seven young Armenian girls were abducted for the King's pleasure; some of them were afterwards compelled to marry Muslims who proceeded to claim what little remained of their relatives' goods.

In 1675 the post of Bishop of Isfahan which had been unoccupied since 1632 was occupied for a short time by a man who was eminently worthy of the task, François Picquet. He had been the

French Consul in Aleppo for many years and had acquired an excellent knowledge of the Levant and its languages. Later he joined the Carmelite order and at the time of his appointment as bishop was Prior of Grimault in Provence. He was 48 at the time of his appointment in 1674 and it took him seven years before he actually reached Isfahan. He immediately asked that a certain Monsignor Pidou be appointed his coadjutor, which was done. Bishop Picquet decided to make his episcopal residence in Hamadan and to this end bought a house and garden there. But he was not to enjoy it for long; in 1685 he died and the house became the subject of prolonged and acrimonious litigation – a sad legacy for such a distinguished man to leave behind him.

Bishop Pidou arrived in Isfahan in 1687 accompanied by three secular priests and two Franciscan tertiaries, all French. This sudden influx was rather too much for the unfortunate Carmelites who were poor and whose common language was Italian. The position was somewhat difficult and Bishop Pidou did not make it any easier by being inclined to push French interests as opposed to the wider interests of the mission as a whole.

Shah Suleiman died in 1694 and his successor, Shah Sultan Hosein (1694–1722), continued in his footsteps and completed the ruin of the kingdom. The end of the Safavi dynasty was in sight. There is a Muslim legend that succinctly sums up the situation. It is said that Solomon, King of the Jews, died standing up while the building of the Temple was in progress. The *jinn* who was helping build the Temple did not know he was dead until worms ate through the staff he was leaning on and he fell to the ground. This legend, says Professor E. G. Browne, 'may well serve as a parable of the century of Safavi rule which followed the death of Shah Abbas I'.

Meanwhile scandals beset the missionaries: two Augustinians became Muslims and were the cause of such scandal that even their fellow-Muslims were disgusted. The Armenians, led by Stephen, the more-than-usually-contentious Bishop of Julfa, attacked the Carmelites in their own house. Finally they had to call on the bodyguard of the Polish Ambassador, Father Zapolski S.J., to protect them. At last they were compelled to leave Julfa, much to the regret of many of the ordinary people. Nevertheless, in 1694 the Carmelites could claim that they had the greatest ever number of missionaries. In the convent in Isfahan they had four Fathers and a lay brother and in Julfa they had five Fathers.

73

In 1707 the arrival of Sieur Jean Fabre as the French Ambassador caused another major scandal. He brought with him his mistress, known to all as 'la nymphe fatale'. He unwisely announced that she was a present from the King of France (Louis XIV) to the Shah. The lady seems to have relished the prospect of becoming Queen of Persia and made no bones about it on the score of religion. When Fabre was poisoned by the Shah, probably with her connivance, she seemed to have some hopes of becoming 'Ambassador' in his place. But by this time the religious and other French authorities were becoming seriously concerned and they joined forces to frustrate her – which they succeded in doing very effectively. Nevertheless, Bishop Pidou had to write to the Sacred Congregation in June 1707: 'The harm which has been caused in Persia by the extravagant proceedings and imprudences of the late Sieur Jean Fabre sent by the King to the Sufi, is only too notorious and public and has been unutterably prejudicial to the honour of France and to the interests of the Catholic religion.'

But all was by no means lost and missionaries are always having to see their words and examples denied by so-called Christians behaving badly. In 1695 the Dominicans who had been in Julfa for many years started building a new church there. It was finally completed in 1705, thanks to the help of two members of the Shariman family, Gaspar and Nazar. The Sharimans were Catholic Armenians who thanks to their contacts with Italy had made a great deal of money which they were always willing to spend on behalf of their adopted Church, to which they stuck loyally through good times and bad. This church still exists today (up to 1935 it was used by the Lazarist mission in Julfa).

The final collapse of the Safavi dynasty came about in a peculiarly terrible way. First, a rebellion broke out in Afghanistan among one of the dominant tribes, the Ghilzai. The Persians, unwilling to let the Georgian troops have a free hand, did not stop the rebellion and in 1719 the Afghans made a raid across the Dasht-e-Lut and attacked Kerman. Nearly two years later they launched a further and more extensive attack. By February 1722 the Afghans had reached Yezd and were moving on towards Isfahan. On 8 March the two armies met at Gulnabad, the Persians were defeated and Isfahan was besieged. The siege lasted until the autumn and only ended when Shah Sultan Hosein abdicated and personally placed the crown on the head of the Afghan usurper, Mir Mahmud. On

24 October Mir Mahmud paraded through the streets of Isfahan so that the populace could see their new Shah. Naturally enough, the Turks took advantage of the Persian weaknesses and by the end of 1725 had occupied much of Western Persia as far south as Hamadan, which they were to hold for the next eight years.

The state of the country obviously discouraged any organised missionary work. The Fathers had retreated to Julfa during the siege and the Polish Jesuit, Father Krusinski, has left a long and vivid account of the history of the period. In 1728 the situation was summed up by the Capuchin Father Dionysius who wrote: 'the mission which many hardships . . . famine, wars and other misfortunes . . . are crushing, if all these storms and commotions are to be weathered, must be aided and provision made for it . . . our Superiors have not given a single reply to my letters for eight years so that I am weighed down by these calamities.' The other orders were all in very much the same state.

The Afghans' rule was short-lived; a new Persian hero arose in time of need. In 1729 the commander-in-chief of the Persian army, Nader Quli Beg, restored Tahmasp, son of Sultan Hosein, to the throne. But Tahmasp was a weakling and in 1736, having conducted a remarkable series of campaigns in which he regained nearly all the territory that Persia had lost, Nader deposed Tahmasp and proclaimed himself Shah.

THE REIGN OF NADER SHAH

The new Shah spent most of his time campaigning far from his capital. After the Afghan invasion, for reasons which are not entirely clear, all non-Muslims were turned out of Isfahan and compelled to live in Julfa. This was not relished by the Armenians who between 1738 and 1740 once again tried to have all the foreign missionaries turned out of the country.

In 1740 Nader Shah, who was by no means an orthodox Muslim, decided that the Bible and the Koran should be translated into Persian. He seems to have had some idea of synthesising the two religions. The Jews were ordered to translate the Old Testament, the Catholics to translate the Gospels and the Armenians the rest of the New Testament. The work was to be finished in six months, so the end product was by no means good. When the translation was complete the translators went to Qazvin to present it to the

Shah, who had given orders that they were to be courteously received. A contemporary account describes what followed: 'When the day appointed for the audience arrived they were all conducted together to the gate of the garden and there made to halt. Every now and then they saw, to their horror, men of all sorts with halters round their necks going in before the Shah. There they were strangled and afterwards dragged out like animals. This spectacle lasted almost an hour during which time eighteen people were strangled.' The two Catholic Fathers were sure that their last hour had come and that they were to receive the crown of martyrdom. Father Leander, whose account has been quoted above, says that they disputed hotly who should have the privilege of going first to his glory. In the event they were to be disappointed for the Shah merely received the translations and dismissed the translators with 100 *tomans* to share between them.

For a few years the missionaries were left in peace, and were disturbed only by the usual feuding with the orthodox Armenians. But in 1745 Nader Shah paid his first visit to Isfahan since his coronation. By this time his greed and megalomania were well advanced and his licence and cruelty knew no bounds. He extracted everything he possibly could from the hapless Armenians and the following year came back for more (it was reported that he robbed them of a further 60,500 *tomans*). But Nader's cruelty was not limited to non-Muslims; it extended to his own people as well and he became universally hated. In 1747 he was assassinated by his own bodyguard to whom he had taken a dislike and was planning to have murdered. One of the Fathers writing at the time said: 'The cause of his end was nothing less than his tyrannical fits, which in the last years of his life it was his whim to indulge to the uttermost'.

THE FINAL FAILURE

With the death of Nader Shah, the precarious peace of the country was shattered and the organised mission of the Catholics ceased to exist. Individual Fathers continued to live and work in the country, but with ever-diminishing support from Rome. In 1753 the rebel Azad Khan entered Isfahan; his troops occupied the Augustinian convent and stabled their horses in the church. Luri and Bakhtiari tribesmen constantly raided the town and the bishop's residence in Hamadan was utterly destroyed. One hundred thousand Persians and most of the Armenians of Julfa took refuge in Baghdad.

Isfahan, which even after the Afghan invasions had retained a population of some 250,000, was now a ghost town with a population of only some 40,000–50,000 people. The country was divided into different areas of influence; in the south, Karim Khan Zand ruled as *Vakil* or representative in Shiraz, and the Qajar tribe was dominant in the north. The author of *A Chronicle of the Carmelites* sums up the situation in this way: 'It appears therefore that it was the renewed struggle and further fighting between the Zands and the Qajars and the disorders and lawlessness that prevailed in the years between Karim Khan Zand's death in 1779 and 1791 which finally ruined the Catholics of Julfa.'

By 1750 the last remaining Augustinian Father had gone; the Jesuits hung on in Julfa and Resht until about 1760 when they handed over to the Capuchins, who had transferred the centre of their missionary work from Persia to Astrakhan in Russia.

In 1770 the mission in Resht was taken over by a wandering priest, Emmanuel Caro, who was born in Mexico. He had previously been in England and Holland on unspecified missions and then went to Russia where he unexpectedly gained the favour of the Empress who sent him to minister to the expatriate community in Resht. After three years he abandoned this task, which can have been by no means arduous, and retired to Shiraz where he apparently earned a precarious living as a doctor.

The Dominicans, first in the field in Persia, lasted longest in Julfa in the person of Father Raymond Berselli who, writing in 1763, reported that there were only twenty-five Catholics left there. The next year he died and was not replaced. Thus ended 250 years of devoted effort with no visible results whatsoever. But one cannot help feeling that in spite of all their mistakes – and the mistakes of those who sent them and burdened them with such impossible tasks – the presence of these devoted men was a good thing for Persia. They made but little impression on the course of history, but for many, many ordinary, helpless people over the years, they provided charity and hope. For the writer, they can all be summed up in the person of Father Aimé Chezaud, the first of the Jesuits, who lived in utter poverty, always sleeping on a mat on the floor and dressing in a short grey habit usually torn and patched and with a worn fur cap on his head. His main diet was bread and wild cherries and his main occupation was the care of the poor. When he died thousands of people of all races and classes attended his funeral. Throughout his long life he was known as *patre-habib*, beloved father, a title he fully deserved.

THE LATER HISTORY OF THE ASSYRIAN CHURCH

In the 150 years that followed the ravages of Timur-e-Lang, the Assyrian Church declined rapidly in numbers and extent. Many of its bishoprics lapsed and it gradually retreated until it was only found in north-western Persia and the mountains of eastern Turkey. A symptom of its weakness may be found in the fact that in 1551 a dispute arose as to the election of a new Patriarch. A group of monks and bishops denied the validity of the hereditary principle, which would make the previous Patriarch's nephew his successor, and chose a monk from the monastery of Rabban Hormizd, John Sulacha by name. In order to support his claims, John Sulacha made contact with Franciscan missionaries who were working in the area and with their help he went to Rome, where he made a Catholic confession of faith to Pope Julius III. On his return he hoped to win over all the Nestorians to his uniate Church, but in this he was unsuccessful. After only two years he was arrested by the governor of Diabekr and put in prison; while there, he was murdered.

The two lines continued to appoint their own Patriarchs. The first three successors of John Sulacha kept in close contact with Rome, but gradually the contacts grew less and less. The last Patriarch we hear of who sent his confession of faith to Rome is Mar Shimun XII in 1670. The other line of succession also soon realised the value of contacts with Rome and they too sent their submission to Rome, which was accepted. The seat of the Patriarch in the John Sulacha line was at Urmiah and that of the original line, whose Patriarch was always known as Mar Elias, was at Mosul.

By the beginning of the eighteenth century both Patriarchs had reverted to their original independent status. Meanwhile, the Metropolitan of Diabekr made his profession of faith to Rome and was appointed Uniate Patriarch of the Chaldees. In 1826 the Mosul Patriarchate again became uniate. As a result from then on there was a Uniate Patriarchate based on Mosul (and later Baghdad) and an independent Patriarchate based on Urmiah (later on Kochanes). It is along this latter line that the present-day Patriarchate is descended and it can fairly claim to be the legitimate heir of the ancient Church – the Assyrian Church of the East.

The Uniate or Chaldean Church in Iran was formally established in Iran in 1581 when the Chaldean Patriarchal see was brought to the monastery of St John near Salmas. The Church today has approximately 14,000 communicant members and is part of the Patriarchate of Babylon. (The present Patriarch is Mar Paulos II who resides in Baghdad.) In Iran there are three Archbishops, all of equal status, and the Church maintains five elementary schools with a total enrolment of about 900 as well as a smaller secondary school. The ancient Assyrian Church of the East still survives and flourishes today although the Patriarch is now resident in America where there is also a large and flourishing body of Assyrian Christians. More than half the Iranian members now live in Tehran and the bulk of the remainder in the Rezaiah area.

The numbers of Assyrians of both branches have been greatly reduced by the aftermath of two World Wars and the migration of many to the United States. They continue, however, to represent a vital strand in the religious life of Iran and are witness to the long-standing existence of Christianity there. (See also Chapter 11.)

THE ROMAN CATHOLICS IN THE 19TH CENTURY

As we have seen, by the second half of the eighteenth century the great Roman Catholic missionary effort in Iran had dwindled almost to nothing. But from 1838 onwards it was to be revived by the devoted, if sometimes misguided, efforts of a French layman, Eugène Boré. Boré was born in Algiers in 1809 and educated in Paris at the *Collège Stanislas*. From 1830 to 1836 he studied oriental languages and became proficient in Arabic, Turkish, Armenian, Persian, Hebrew and Syriac. In 1837 the *Académie des Inscriptions* sent him on a scientific mission to Persia.

While he was in Isfahan he was struck by the need for a Western-style school and was also imbued with a burning desire to spread the Catholic faith. In one of his letters of this time he wrote: 'Aujourd'hui le premier devoir du voyageur chrétien est de s'élever autant qu'il est en lui à la dignité de missionaire.' He attempted to open a school in Julfa where he claimed there were only 1,800 inhabitants and 40 priests. Naturally this move was not appreciated by the Armenians who still remembered the struggles of an earlier epoch.

In November 1838 Boré arrived in Tabriz, where he felt that

79

there was the same pressing need for a school on European lines. In a letter to his family he wrote: 'La jeunesse de Perse est avide d'instruction elle recueillera avec avidité toutes les connaissances qui lui seront apportées d'Europe.'

In February 1839 he wrote to the *Ministère d'Instruction Publique* urging them to start a French language college or a university in Tabriz. Meanwhile he himself made a start and with typical Gallic enthusiasm he wrote to his family: 'Je ne désespère pas d'établir à Tauris un petit Collège de France.' He soon gathered some pupils around him and before long had fourteen students: eleven Muslims and three Armenians. He submitted them to a comprehensive course of instruction on French lines and made them do gymnastic exercises and accompany him on long walks.

In 1840 Boré accompanied the French Ambassador to Isfahan where the Shah was in residence. They had an audience with the Shah who issued a firman that Catholics should have freedom of conscience, could open schools, contract marriages among themselves and carry on trade.

Before he left Persia Boré had contacted the Lazarist Fathers of St Vincent de Paul asking them to help in continuing the missionary work which he had begun. The first recruit, Père Fornier, arrived in Persia in 1840 and worked there until his death eighteen years later. In the following year he was joined by two more: Darnis and Cluzel. The latter was to spend many years in Persia and rose to the rank of Monsignor.

The missionaries soon separated; Darnis went to Urmiah, Cluzel to Isfahan, while Fornier remained in Tabriz. Boré remained for a while with Cluzel in Isfahan. But they aroused great hostility; parents who sent their children to the Roman Catholic school were excommunicated from the Armenian Church, and the bishop rode round on his horse urging his flock to have nothing to do with the missionaries. Later in this year Boré returned to France. We hear of him again as French Consul in Jerusalem where his proselytising zeal again got him into trouble. He then moved on to Constantinople where he taught in the Lazarist college. In 1850 he was ordained priest and entered the novitiate of the Lazarist Fathers. On taking his final vows he was appointed head of the College of Bebek in Constantinople where for fifteen years he was instrumental in spreading Catholic and French influence throughout the Levant. In 1866 he returned to France to become Secretary of the order, and in 1874 he became its Superior General. He died suddenly in 1878. The educational work which he started in Iran has grown and the numerous French educational establishments (of which mention will be made later) have been potent influences for good in the educational development of Iran, and they all owed their origin in part at least to his efforts.

Boré has often been criticised for his relentless proselytising, but he was not by any means completely devoid of ecumenical spirit and was as tolerant in his rooted opposition to other Christian bodies as his zeal and the prevailing atmosphere in his own Church permitted. He wrote warmly of the work of the American missionaries :

'Nous nous réjouissons en Notre Seigneur Jesus-Christ de l'œuvre qu'ils ont entreprise dans plusieurs contrées depuis le commencement de ce siècle. Ils ont traduit les Saintes Ecritures dans les idiomes les moins connus, ils ont colporté et semé des milliers de Bibles et d'Evangiles de l'orient au couchant, ils ont ouvert des écoles qui habituent le peuple à apprécier l'instruction . . . Certes nous glorifions Dieu qu'ils aient poussé tant d'âmes à moitié chemin de la vérité.'

Nevertheless the conflict between the sects continued and Boré left bitter memories. The anti-Catholic cause was espoused by the Russian Consul, M. de Meden, who was of French Protestant extraction. He intrigued against the mission in Isfahan to such an extent that, in spite of the Shah's firman, Cluzel had to leave. When the Lazarists began work they tactlessly (one would think) dedicated their church to 'Marie, mère de Dieu', which naturally enough caused much resentment. Cluzel and Darnis were ordered to leave the country and for a short time actually did retreat over the border into Russia. The mission property in Urmiah was saved from destruction by its being promptly occupied by Monsieur Nicolas, the dragoman of the French Embassy. The priests soon returned, but were not allowed to go back to Urmiah, so they settled in Khosrova, where a seminary was founded which did great work in training indigenous priests.

In 1856 the Soeurs de la Charité were invited from Constantinople by Cluzel. They had previously been tending the wounded during the Crimean War, and were now free to move on. Eight came in the first group under the leadership of Soeur Philomène de Cousebouc. They soon started educational and dispensary work and were granted a subsidy of 200 *tomans* a year by Nasr-ud-din Shah. By 1883 there were twenty-three Sisters located in Khosrova, Urmiah and Tehran. Darnis, the head of the mission, died in 1858 and was succeeded by Cluzel. In 1859 there were three Lazarist Fathers in Khosrova, supervising the seminary, and six schools in the plain of Salmas and eleven schools in the plain of Urmiah, with four more Fathers located in Urmiah itself.

In 1866 a bad typhus epidemic caused the deaths of a number of the Fathers and the work began to decline to such an extent that in 1870 everything had to be abandoned and work was not started again until 1874. From then on the work continued steadily. By 1892 there were two seminaries in Urmiah, a teacher-training college with boarding facilities for training village teachers, and forty-five village schools in the surrounding area. At Khosrova there was a strong parochial life; youth work and charitable work amongst the poor was carried on. All this work has now lapsed with the exception of a well-attended girls' school run by the Sisters of Charity in Rezaiah (as Urmiah is now called).

Soon after Cluzel succeeded Darnis as head of the mission three Assyrians went to France and after a short novitiate joined the missionary Fathers in Iran. The most famous of these was Père Paul Bedjan, who proved to be a notable scholar and whose editions of ancient Syriac texts have been widely admired.

In 1872 The Apostolic Delegation for Persia was created and Cluzel was recalled to Paris where he was consecrated Archbishop of Heraclea. He then returned to Persia with the titles of Apostolic Delegate for Persia and Administrator of the Diocese of Isfahan. Cluzel was a man of commanding presence and soon made his influence widely felt. He was honoured by the Shah, who made him a member of the Order of the Lion and the Sun. He settled in Urmiah where he engaged in extensive building, including a fine cathedral in Urmiah and numerous chapels and oratories in the surrounding villages. He died in 1882. After a short interregnum he was succeeded by Monsignor Lesné, Archbishop of Philippolis, who had come to Persia as a missionary some seven years previously.

Work in Tehran

In 1861 the authorities, recognising the lack of pastoral care for Catholics in Tehran, sent two missionaries there, Père Varese and Père Plagnard. The former very soon had to retire owing to ill-health but Plagnard remained and soon rallied the small Catholic community around him and formed a congregation. In 1862 he opened a boys' school and in 1866 he began to build a church. This was completed the following year and the first mass was celebrated in it on Christmas Day 1867. In 1892 a small boarding department mainly for orphans was added to the school. Today the Collège St Louis is a flourishing boys' school with over 600 pupils.

The Sisters of Charity came to Tehran in 1875 and soon started a dispensary, a children's home and a small girls' school. By 1896 they had two schools – one in the Darvazeh Qazvin district and one in the Darvazeh Dowlat area. Today they are responsible for the École Jeanne d'Arc which has 1,600 pupils. They also engage in charitable work among the poor.

Work in Tabriz
The work in Tabriz lapsed when the town ceased to be the important commercial and diplomatic centre that it was when Boré came there. Activities were not restarted there until 1901 when Père Malaval and Père Mas came there and engaged in pastoral and educational work. In 1930 a church was built. Today, in addition to a small parochial ministry, a boys' school with 400 pupils and a girls' school with 450 pupils are maintained.

Work in Isfahan
Work in Julfa Isfahan started again with the arrival of Père Émile Demuth in 1903. Three more Fathers joined him during the next year and a school was opened for Armenian children and an Armenian printing press was set up. In 1925 the mission was transferred to Isfahan proper, and the printing press abandoned. Today there is a small parochial ministry and a boys' school under Père Zwick with 150 pupils and a girls' school with 800 pupils. This latter is run by Sisters of Charity who arrived in Julfa in 1904 and moved with the school to its present location in Isfahan in 1937.

OTHER CATHOLIC GROUPS

The Little Brothers and Sisters of Jesus
Following in the footsteps of Père Charles de Foucauld, whom they try to emulate, they work in leprosariums in Tabriz and Meshed; four Sisters are working amongst the poor in Tehran. They belong to the Uniate Chaldean diocese in Iran.

Dominicans
Towards the end of 1933, Father Cyprian Rice (a former member of the British diplomatic service in Iran) and Father Dominic Blencowe came to Iran and founded a house in Shiraz. Father Rice spoke fluent Persian having been a pupil of Browne and Nicholson. He composed a tract on the person of Christ and translated the prayer book into Persian. He also made a deep study of Persian Sufism. This resulted in the publication of his book, *The Persian Sufis*, which was the fruit of his long friendship with the venerable Ni'matullahi Dervish Sheikh Shamsul 'Urafa. His stay in Persia was short owing to the hostility and suspicion which his presence aroused at that time and because he received inadequate support from his own competent religious authorities. After only eight months in Shiraz they were compelled to leave, but Father Rice continued his studies and remained deeply interested in Persian Sufism.

In 1962 the Papal nuncio in Iran invited Fathers from the Dominican province of Ireland to come and work in Iran. Father William Barden, the present Apostolic Administrator, arrived in May 1962. In 1967 the Fathers moved into a new building complex especially designed for them. It includes a small modern church, a university-student centre and a house for the fathers.

The Salesians
The first group of four Salesian Fathers came to Iran in February 1937; two of them, Father Streit and Brother Taliano, are still in Iran. They came originally to take charge of the Consolata Church and to minister to the Italian immigrants who were numerous at that time. Father del Mistro arrived the following year and is still working in Iran; his Persian version of the four Gospels is shortly to be published and he has also prepared (and hopes to publish) a large Persian-Italian dictionary.

In 1944 Father del Mistro opened a small boys' school with the name of the Andisheh-Don Bosco School. This school has flourished until now twenty members of the order are at work in it, twelve of whom are priests. The school has no less than 1,200 pupils at the present time. The school also possesses land and buildings at Now Shahr on the Caspian Sea where a summer camp is held every year for about ninety boys. Since 1934 the Salesians have also had charge of all the Catholics in the oilfields area of Khuzistan.

Part Three

THE PROTESTANT ENDEAVOUR AND THE FOUNDING OF INDIGENOUS CHURCHES

Chapter Eight

THE FORERUNNERS

The history of Iran in the nineteenth century is largely the history of the rivalry between the Great Powers, first Russia and Great Britain, with France joining in a little later. As the century passed most of the other European powers joined in the scramble for concessions and other advantages that could be gained from the perennially impoverished country.

In 1801 an Indian army captain, John Malcolm, was sent by the Governor-General of Bengal to negotiate a treaty with Iran, aimed at curbing the power of the Afghan leader, Zaman Shah, who was thought to constitute a threat to India's northern borders. The following year Napoleon's first envoy, the Armenian Mir David Melik Shahnazar, arrived in Tehran. In 1807 Napoleon conceived the idea that it might be possible to attack India via Iran and so signed the Treaty of Finkenstein with her, offering an alliance to protect Iran from Britain and Russia.

In 1813 after a disastrous campaign against Russia, Iran was compelled to sign the humiliating Treaty of Gulistan – abandoning her claims to Georgia and accepting the southern shores of the Caspian Sea as her boundary, thus giving up the important town of Baku. In 1828 after even more disastrous defeats at the hands of the Russians, Iran again had to submit and sign the Treaty of Turkomanchai, in which the river Aras was finally accepted as the northern boundary of Persian Azerbaijan. The 'Great Game'* between Britain and Russia had begun. Iran's only weapon in all the subsequent manœuvres was her gift of *chuneh* or bargaining and her ability to play one country off against another; which she did with consummate skill.

But even before politicians and diplomats had begun to be con-

* This was the British way of referring to the battle of wits and espionage between England and Russia for the control of Central Asia; later immortalised by Kipling in *Kim*.

cerned with Persia, interest had been aroused amongst antiquarians and literary men. Anquétil du Perron's work on the Zoroastrians in 1771, Rückert's translations from the Persian and Goethe's *West-Östlicher Divan* all made people aware of the country at the end of the eighteenth and the beginning of the nineteenth century. In England the increasing importance of her Indian possessions and the discovery that Persian was widely spoken there, aroused great interest in Persian as a language. Claudius Buchanan underlined its importance when he wrote :

> The Persian language is known far beyond the limits of Persia proper. It is spoken in all the Musulman courts in India and is the usual language of judicial procedure under the British government in Hindustan. It is next in importance to the Arabic and Chinese languages in regard to the extent of the territory through which it is spoken, being generally understood from Calcutta to Damascus.

The Moravians

The earliest Protestant missionary effort that had any part of Iran for its objective, seems to have been the heroic effort of two German doctors, C. F. W. Hoecker and J. Rueffer, missionaries of the United Brethren or Moravians. These two pioneers left Germany in 1747 with the intention of going to Yezd to conduct a mission among the Zoroastrians there. When they arrived at Aleppo, they put themselves under the protection of the British Consul, who advised them that the situation in Persia was far too unsetttled for them to be able to proceed.

But they were not the kind of men to be deterred by the prospect of dangers or difficulties and so on 27 August 1747 they left Aleppo with a caravan of 1,500 camels destined, as they thought, for Baghdad. However, after they had been travelling for some time, they found that the caravan was going to Basra, so they parted company with it. Accompanied by only four Jews they journeyed on, reaching Baghdad on 12 September, and the Persian border two days later. The governor of the border town, Shahmakhan, in Persia, had had his eyes put out by Nader Shah. When he heard that two foreign doctors had arrived in the town he asked them to help him, but they could only tell him that a miracle would be needed to restore his sight. Another patient, whom they were able to treat more successfully, gave them two donkeys for their onward journey. On 21 October they set out again for Isfahan, with a caravan of 600 people. Two days out from Shahmakhan they were attacked by a band of Kurdish robbers. Both the missionaries were stripped of everything they possessed, even their clothes. In this condition they had to walk fifteen miles in the heat of the day to the nearest town. Here they found a friendly Persian who took them in and gave them clothes and a little money. It took them nine more days to reach Isfahan and on the journey they suffered terribly from hunger and the great cold at night.

In Isfahan they were befriended by the British agent, who told them that the state of the country was so uncertain that it would be madness for them to try to get to Yezd. However, early in the New Year, they set out once more and were again robbed of everything they possessed. They struggled on and after great hardships eventually made their way to Bushire, where the kindhearted agent of the Dutch East India Company enabled them to leave the country and get to Basra. From there they made their way to Egypt, where Rueffer died as a result of his privations, while Hoecker proceeded to England alone, arriving early in 1750. His missionary zeal was unabated and he soon left for Abyssinia where he had even more hair-raising adventures and an equal lack of success.

Henry Martyn
In 1800 Wellesley, the Governor-General of Bengal, encouraged the founding of a college in Calcutta for the training of civil servants for India. The college was known from its location as Fort William College; its first Provost was the veteran East India Company's chaplain, David Brown, and the Vice-Provost was Claudius Buchanan. William Carey, the famous Baptist missionary from the Danish settlement at Serampore, was the Professor of Sanscrit. Although no missionaries were allowed into any part of British India until 1813, the college had a department for the translation of the Scriptures into oriental languages. The first versions of any of the Gospels in Persian or Hindustani which were printed in India came from the college printing press. The earliest versions in Persian were issued under the guidance of Colonel Colebrook. Later the control of the translation work was undertaken by one who in his very short life was to become famous in the history of Christianity in Iran : Henry Martyn.

Henry Martyn was born in the Cornish town of Truro in 1781. His parents belonged to the prosperous middle class, and were disposed to be religious; his father had been greatly influenced by the evangelical preacher Samuel Walker and later by John Wesley. Martyn was educated at the local grammar school, and in 1797 left home for the first time to go up to the University of Cambridge. Here he became a member of St John's College, and although up to that time his education had been entirely classical, he decided to read mathematics. While he was at Cambridge he experienced some form of religious conversion and came under the influence of Charles Simeon, Fellow of King's College and Vicar of Holy Trinity Cambridge. Simeon was a keen evangelical and as such was not everywhere popular; his evening services, which Martyn began to attend, were deemed unnecessary and were often interrupted by undergraduate ribaldry.

In 1801 Martyn took his degree and rather to his surprise found himself a Senior Wrangler. In 1802 he offered to the recently established Society for Missions to Africa and the East (later known as the Church Missionary Society) and was accepted. In 1803 he was ordained at Ely and became Simeon's curate in the little village of Lolworth. In addition to his clerical duties, which he took very seriously, and those incumbent upon him as a Fellow of his college, he also made time to study oriental languages and to gain that knowledge and love of Persian literature (especially the poems of Sa'di) which were to be so very useful to him later on.

A change in his father's fortunes put an end to Martyn's hopes of a missionary career; his father lost a lot of money and Martyn became financially responsible for his unmarried sister Sally – a responsibility he could never have discharged on a missionary salary. On Simeon's advice he offered to the East India Company as a chaplain and thanks to the interest shown by a director, Charles Grant, he was accepted, and in July 1805, having been priested, he set sail for India, where he arrived nine months later.

In Calcutta he stayed with Brown, the Provost of Fort William College, and settled down to help in the work of the Church and to improve his knowledge of Persian and Hindustani. In September 1806 he was appointed chaplain at Dinapore near Patna and in June of the following year was asked to help in the translations of the New Testament then being made into Arabic, Persian and Hindustani. This work had already been started at Fort William

College by two remarkable men, Mirza Fitrat of Benares and Aga Sabat, an Arab from Baghdad. Sabat was to become Martyn's chief helper for the Persian version, even though he was an Arab and had only been in Persia for ten years. He was an extremely violent and unstable man with a loud voice and an explosive temperament, which proved a great trial to the sensitive and somewhat reserved young Englishman.

In 1809 Martyn was transferred to Cawnpore where his physical weakness soon became evident. He arrived there seriously ill and stayed for some time in the house of Mr and Mrs Sherwood, who nursed him for several months. Mrs Sherwood was later to gain fame as the author of *The Fairchild Family* and other children's books. In her *Autobiography* she gives a moving picture of the young Martyn – so pious and so earnest, and yet so cheerful and such good fun that everyone loved him.

In 1810 his health became so bad that he was given indefinite leave of absence from his post in order to complete his translations of the New Testament. When he arrived in Calcutta he was told that Sabat's translation of the New Testament which had just been printed was deemed unsatisfactory and needed complete revision. He therefore modified his original plan of going to Arabia to search for early manuscripts of the Gospels and decided to go first to Persia for a short time to carry out the revision.

Having made the necessary preparations in Calcutta and obtained some letters of introduction to Armenians in Persia from their co-religionists there, he reached Bombay, where he met the great John Malcolm, who was then engaged on writing his *History of Persia*. Malcolm was very helpful to Martyn, presenting him with a Chaldee Missal and giving him introductions to various important people in Persia. Malcolm was much impressed by the earnest young man and writing to the British Ambassador in Persia, Sir Gore Ouseley, about him, he said:

His intention is, I believe, to go by Shiraz, Isfahan and Kerman-shah to Baghdad and to endeavour on that route to discover some ancient copies of the Gospel, which he and many other saints are persuaded lie hidden in the mountains of Persia. Mr Martyn also expects to improve himself as an oriental scholar; he is already an excellent one. His knowledge of Arabic is superior to that of any Englishman in India. He is altogether a very learned and cheerful man, but a great enthusiast in his holy calling.

Early in 1811 Martyn set sail on the *Benares,* which was going to the Persian Gulf on a punitive expedition against the pirates there. On 21 May the ship reached Bushire, where Martyn left it. As soon as possible he acquired Persian clothes and all the other necessaries for the journey across the mountains to Shiraz, which he reached on Sunday, 9 June.

In Shiraz he stayed with a wealthy merchant, Jaffar Ali Khan, to whom Malcolm had given him an introduction. He quickly settled down with his faithful Armenian servant, Zachary, and found himself a language assistant in the person of Mirza Seid Ali. He hoped to complete his work before the autumn and then to move on in search of Arabic manuscripts. But his presence in the city was a source of unending speculation for the population, most of whom tried to see him in person, so Martyn had to cope with an unending stream of visitors of all kinds. Opinions as to the reason for his being there varied; some thought that he was a sincere seeker after religious truth who had come to Shiraz in order to study and adopt Islam. Others, more worldly-wise, but just as far from the truth, decided that he was a British spy, who had come to prepare the way for 5,000 British soldiers from India to come and take over the city. Gradually his callers realised that they had something different on their hands and that here was a deeply convinced Christian who was well able to give reasons for his faith and who could speak in love and charity and with great patience to all who came to him to discuss religion. His fervent devotion to Jesus made a great and lasting impression, so much so that the *mujtaheds* or religious leaders wrote tracts refuting his arguments and engaged in long verbal contests with him.

As the winter drew near, he renewed his plans for moving on to Baghdad, and his translator Mirza Seid Ali agreed to go with him. But unsettled conditions and the winter weather made him decide to stay on in Shiraz until the spring. By the beginning of 1812 he seems to have realised that the completion of the translation of the New Testament into Persian was going to be his most important work. On 1 January 1812 he wrote in his journal:

> Spared by mercy to see the beginning of another year; transported in safety to Shiraz, I have been led by the particular providence of God to undertake a work, the idea of which never entered my mind, but which has gone on without material interruption and is now nearly finished. To all appearance the present

year will be more perilous than any I have seen, but if I live to complete the Persian New Testament my life after that will be of less importance.

As time went on he became increasingly conscious of his physical weakness and he must have had a strong presentiment that he was going to die. Nevertheless, he continued his work of translation, which was continually interrupted by long and exhausting debates with Muslim religious leaders, both Orthodox and Sufi, until by 24 February 1812 the translation was complete. All that remained to be done was to send it to the calligraphers to be written out in a form suitable for presentation to the Shah. This task was completed by the beginning of May and on the twelfth of that month Martyn set out for Tabriz, intending to give the manuscript to the British Ambassador who had agreed to present it formally to the Shah. Twelve days' hard riding brought him to Isfahan and a further eight days' to Tehran. Here the party was delayed because no muleteers could be found to take them on to Tabriz. Martyn became increasingly conscious that every moment was precious to him, so when he learnt that the Shah was in residence in one of his palaces near Tehran, he decided to act himself. He had a letter of introduction to the Vizier but when he called on him he was treated with contempt and found himself engaged in a long and acrimonious conversation with a number of *mullahs*, a conversation which grew so heated that at one point it seemed as if Martyn's life might be in danger.

Disappointed in this hope, Martyn saw that the only thing to do was to press on to Tabriz. On the journey both Martyn and his English companion, Canning, became seriously ill and they did not arrive in Tabriz until 7 July. The Ambassador immediately took Martyn into his house and gave him every possible care and attention. He promised to present the copies of the New Testament to the Shah with all the necessary formalities to ensure a respectful reception. The work was in due course formally received by Fath Ali Shah and in a letter of thanks he said: 'If it please the most merciful God we shall command the select servants who are admitted to our presence, to read to us the above mentioned book from the beginning to the end.' These copies have been lost, but other copies given to Sir Gore Ouseley were transmitted by him to the Russian Bible Society, which promptly printed them, thus securing for St Petersburg the honour of being the first to print this most famous of all translations of the New Testament into Persian. A copy of this first edition is a proud possession of his old church, Holy Trinity, Cambridge.

Martyn's state of health was so obviously desperate that he was persuaded to apply to the East India Company for leave of absence and permission to proceed to England. On 12 September he set out from Tabriz. The country between there and Constantinople, some 1,500 miles, was in a very unsettled state and all travellers were liable to attack by Kurdish and other bandits. Martyn's party was led by a Tartar named Hassan, who was anxious to complete the journey as quickly as possible, and gave no consideration to his master's state of health, driving him on relentlessly until he was utterly exhausted.

Only one diversion is recorded; that was a visit paid to the Armenian Patriarch or Catholicos at Echmiadzin. Martyn always had a special affection for the Armenians, and they for him. A young monk who met him on this visit, long afterwards recalled his appearance, saying he was 'of a very delicate frame, thin and not quite of the middle stature, a beardless youth with a countenance beaming with so much benignity as bespeaks an errand of Divine Love'.

The last entry in Martyn's journal is dated 6 October and includes these words: 'No horses being to be had, I had an unexpected repose. I sat in the orchard and thought with sweet comfort and peace of my God; in solitude my Company, my Friend and Comforter. . . .' Six days later he gave his Armenian servant Sergius all his papers and told him to deliver them to Isaac Morier, the British Consul in Constantinople. Some six weeks later Sergius arrived there and brought the sad news that his master had died at Tokat on 6 October and had been buried there by Armenian monks. Visitors to this little provincial Turkish town can see his tombstone, which is preserved in the local museum.

Martyn was one of those rare Christians who leave an ineffaceable impression of goodness on all whom they meet. Joseph Wolff (about whom more will be heard shortly) visited Shiraz in 1824 and found many who remembered Martyn with great affection. Even the servant who kept his house, Wolff says, spoke well of him; another recalled him as being 'a man who lived close to God'. In January 1825 Wolff was in Isfahan where he met Martyn's servant, Zachary, who said that Martyn 'was like an angel'. In the same year Wolff sent out to various people a questionnaire that included the question: 'What impression do you believe has Henry Martyn made on the minds of the Persians?' One reply to this question has come down to us; that of the British Minister, Sir John McNeill, who answered:

> Henry Martyn produced on Persia a greater impression than any other man could now hope to do, for he was not only admirably calculated for the undertaking, but he was perhaps the first Christian divine, who showed himself superior to the Persians in all the learning on which they most value themselves. I doubt whether Martyn made many converts, but he elicited a spirit of inquiry and discussion, that had not existed before his time, and he taught the Persians to respect a religion that instilled into its votaries the lofty principles of virtue and benevolence, which they admired in him.

Horatio Southgate, wandering in the bazaars of Khoy in 1837, was invited to drink tea with a Persian. In discussion it came out that the Persian had not only read Martyn's translation of the New Testament, but also believed him to have been personally a good man. And in the 1860s a missionary in Algeria came across a desert Sheikh who possessed a carefully-guarded copy of Martyn's Persian New Testament, not knowing what it was, but only that it had been given to his father by its author, a young foreigner, many years before when the father had visited Shiraz on his way back from the pilgrimage to Mecca. Justin Perkins, the founder of the American mission in Persia, was fond of quoting a remark of Martyn's which can serve as the final word: 'Even if I should never see a native converted', he used to say, 'God may design by my patience and continuance in the work, to encourage future missionaries.' They have indeed been encouraged by his example.

Joseph Wolff

The next figure to appear on the missionary scene is about as different from Henry Martyn in background, upbringing and character as can well be imagined. But if they had ever met they would surely have recognised each other as kindred spirits and loyal servants of one Master.

Joseph Wolff was born the son of a Rabbi in Bavaria in 1796.

As a small boy he became interested in Christianity and used to visit secretly the local Lutheran pastor. As a young man he decided to go to the fountain-head, Rome, where he entered a seminary to train for the priesthood. But he soon found himself unable to accept all the Roman doctrine, so, after writing a frank letter to the Pope, he left. In 1819 he arrived in England, still seeking a form of Christianity to which he could give his full allegiance. Soon after his arrival he attended an Anglican service at the Jews' Chapel in Palestine Place and was deeply impressed. The chapel was run by an Anglican missionary society, the London Society for Promoting Christianity among the Jews (CMJ). The Society, which had been founded some ten years earlier, already had a number of missionaries in Europe and the Near East.

Wolff had found what he was looking for and with characteristic impetuousness applied to the Society to be taken on as a missionary. He was accepted and after some time at Cambridge where, like Henry Martyn, he came under the benign influence of Charles Simeon, he was sent on a tour of the Middle East. His position was that of a missionary explorer and traveller and he held and executed a roving commission on behalf of the Society; and rove he certainly did. Between January 1821 and November 1824 he travelled all over the Middle East, visiting the Jewish communities in Malta, Alexandria, Cairo, Sinai, Lebanon, Jerusalem, Damascus, Mardin, Mosul, Baghdad and Basra. In November 1824 he arrived in Bushire and was in Kazerun just in time to be greeted by an earthquake. Later he visited Shiraz and Isfahan and then Kashan, Tehran and Tabriz. In all these places he met and discussed Christianity with both Jews and Muslims. His energy was boundless; on one Sunday in Tabriz he relates that he preached non-stop from 10 a.m. to 6 p.m. in six languages: Russian, Italian, French, German, English and Syriac. On his way out of Persia he visited the Nestorian Christians around Urmiah and Khosrova in North-Western Persia and brought back a very valuable Syriac version of the Pentateuch, which was printed by the British and Foreign Bible Society.

He came back to England full of enthusiasm for missions in Persia and with great ideas for the founding of a number of schools there. As a first step towards the realisation of this plan, he arranged for the visit of a learned Jew, Mirza Ibrahim, with a view to training him to run the first of these schools. But nothing came of the plan.

In 1830 he was off on his travels again and once more visited Persia. In Shusha near the border he met Zaremba, Dittrich and Pfander of the Basel mission (see p. 100), and in Tabriz he met a Pole, Chodzko, attached to the Russian Embassy, who spoke very highly of Pfander as being 'the only Protestant who in later times has travelled in Persia and Mesopotamia as a true missionary'.

After visiting Tehran, where he met some of the *mullahs* who had been engaged in controversy with Henry Martyn, he went on to Khorassan. On the way, near Torbat Heidari, he was robbed by bandits, who only spared his life when the Jews of the town paid a handsome ransom for him. From there he went on to Bokhara, Balkh, Afghanistan, India, Goa, Abyssinia and the Hejaz. Throughout his journeys he wore the full canonical dress of a clergyman of the Church of England and fully earned the description of him given by his first biographer, Lewis Way:

> a man to whom a floor of brick is a featherbed, and a box is a bolster, who makes or finds a friend in the persecutor of his former or his present faith; who can conciliate a Pasha, or confute a Patriarch; who travels without a guide, speaks without an interpreter, can live without food and pay without money, forgiving all the insults he meets with and forgetting all the flattery he receives; who knows little of worldly conduct and yet accommodates himself to all men without giving offence to any. Such a man and such and more is Wolff.

Wolff's later life cannot concern us here, fascinating though it is. Those who are interested can read more about him in his own journals and in Sir Fitzroy Maclean's book, *A Person From England*.

Jacob Samuel

Between the departure of Wolff and the arrival of the regular CMJ missionaries in 1844, another strange and somewhat elusive figure flits across the scene in the person of the Reverend Jacob Samuel. He published a number of works from which the following information is derived, but his style is strong on pieties and curiously weak on facts and the sequence of events is by no means made clear, and he says nothing about his origins or early life.

But it seems that in 1831, as a result of receiving some money from a charitable lady, he was enabled to embark at Greenock for

Calcutta, where he arrived in February 1831 intending to carry on a mission to the Jews of India. He soon managed to gain the interest of a number of Christians and a committee was formed under the chairmanship of Archdeacon (later Bishop) Corrie, which appointed Samuel 'Missionary of the Society for Promoting Christianity among the Jews in India'. But in October of that year he tells us that he was appointed to the Marine Chapel in Calcutta where he ministered to the sailors and soldiers passing through the city. It was not, apparently, until 1834 that he started his work by visiting the Jews in Cochin. In 1835 he went on a missionary tour to the Jews in Baghdad and Arabia and in 1836 he visited Shiraz. In 1837 he was in Tehran preparing to visit the Jews in Daghestan in Georgia, whom he was convinced were the remnants of the lost ten tribes of Israel. In 1837 also he was appointed the British and Foreign Bible Society's agent in Persia and the adjoining countries. In 1840 he published a book to prove his point about the lost ten tribes and in the same year a London auxiliary of the Indian Society was formed, with the title of 'The British Society for Promoting the Spiritual Welfare of the Jews throughout India, Persia and Arabia in Aid of the India Association Established in Bombay'. I have a note of a book by him entitled *Brief Narrative of His Proceedings in Persia etc. 1836–8* (*Bombay* 1838) but there is no copy in the British Museum and I have not seen it. In 1844 he published in Edinburgh a journal of a *Missionary Tour Through the Deserts of Arabia to Baghdad*. On the title page the author describes himself as 'Late senior missionary to the Jews for India, Persia and Arabia . . . principal missionary to the Jewish Scheme in Connexion with the Church of Scotland'. But the tour concerned seems to be that of 1835.

The Edinburgh and the Basel Missionaries

The Edinburgh Missionary Society founded in 1796 (from 1821 onwards it was known as the Scottish Missionary Society) and the Basel Mission were two other societies also at work at this time. The Edinburgh Missionary Society started work in the Caucasus at Karass in 1803 after a *ukase* had been issued by Czar Alexander commending their work and giving them the right to baptise converts. The work started with three missionaries (one of whom was a converted African) and three more joined in 1805. The work mainly consisted of teaching the natives various trades and of printing tracts and Bible portions in Turkish, Persian and the various other languages of the area (which came to include that part of Persia ceded by her to Russia in 1813 and 1828).

In 1816 the centre of the work and the printing press were moved to Astrakhan and the New Testament in Azerbaijan Turki was printed there. The annual report of the mission for this year records that the translation was very well received and many of the Persian merchants who visited the town took it to Darband, Shirvan and even to Isfahan. The same report announces the imminent arrival of a missionary 'who will devote himself chiefly to the Persian language'; this was the great Doctor William Glen who arrived in 1817 and devoted the best part of his life to the translation of the Bible into Persian (see Appendix). The mission encountered many difficulties and the fact that they had Russian protection did not endear them to the local population, who disliked the Russians. But they continued to print and disseminate tracts far and wide and since Astrakhan was a focal point for traffic from north to south as well as from east to west, they had frequent contact with pilgrims from Bokhara, Khiva, Samarkand and Afghanistan.

In 1820 the mission received a letter from a Captain Gordon in Tabriz, urging them to come to Persia; in June of the same year he wrote again from Isfahan saying that he had distributed some of their Christian tracts quite freely in the bazaar and concluded: 'you little think how generally the English *Mullah* Martyn is known throughout Persia and with what affection his memory is cherished.'

In the report for the year 1822–3, the conversion of Mirza Muhammad Ali, the son of a qazi (judge) who was the son of Fath Ali Shah's Prime Minister, is reported from Darband. The conversion of a Persian Muslim of good birth caused quite a stir; when the missionaries wanted to baptise him, the local Orthodox bishop objected. But they got permission from the Minister of Religion in St Petersburg, and the service was performed by Dr Glen in English, Turkish and Persian. The young man took the name of Alexander Kazem-Beg and was afterwards compelled to enter the Russian civil service and attend the University of Omsk.

Kazem-Beg later became a lecturer in Arabic at Kasan University and was one of the founders of oriental studies there. He was later transferred to St Petersburg, where he founded, with A. O. Much-linski, the School of Oriental Studies in the University. The remains of his manuscripts including his polemical writings in Persian on behalf of Christianity are preserved in the library there.

Partly as a result of Russian hostility and partly as a result of their disappointment at the slowness of the Muslims to respond, the Scottish missionaries gradually came to the conclusion that they were not in the right place. So, when in 1822 a group of missionaries from the Basel Missionary Society arrived, they gladly handed over their work to them. Dittrich and Zaremba were the founders of this mission and in 1823 they were joined by C. G. Pfander and Friedrich Haas, both of whom were to spend a number of years in Persia. The Basel mission originally intended to devote itself to a group of emigrant Moravians from Germany who had formed a colony near Astrakhan. But such keen missionaries as Haas and Pfander soon wanted to tackle the local inhabitants and a new station was opened at Shusha, only two days' journey from the Persian frontier.

In 1827 the Scottish missionaries (with the exception of Glen and one other) all withdrew and sold the mission property at Astrakhan to the Basel missionaries. Glen remained on there for many years under the auspices of the British and Foreign Bible Society to complete his Persian translation of the Bible. Pfander also engaged in literary work and made frequent stays in Persia to perfect his knowledge of the language and to correct his translations of the tracts he had written. In 1832 Haas settled in Tabriz where he opened a school under a government *firman*, where he had twenty 'children of the more respectable inhabitants'. Both he and Pfander made frequent journeys distributing tracts and Pfander gained a great reputation as a fearless preacher. Pfander remained in Persia until 1840 when he was finally compelled to leave. He promptly joined the cms, along with several other of the Basel missionaries, and went to India where his Persian experience stood him in good stead. In 1854 he took part with T. V. French in the famous open discussion with the *mullahs* of Agra which resulted in the conversion of two of their number and the foundation of a Christian community in that place. Pfander was the author of a number of tracts, one of which (the *Mizan al Haqq* or *Balance of Truth*) is still in use to this day. One of the missionaries who went with Pfander to India was C. E. Hoernle who was the father of E. F. Hoernle, the first Anglican medical missionary to Persia (see p. 150).

One other strange figure flits briefly and bravely across the scene at about this time – Anthony Norris Groves, who is remembered today chiefly as instrumental with J. N. Darby in founding the sect of the Plymouth Brethren. He was a brilliant young man who from the age of 19 onwards earned a good living as a successful dentist in Exeter. He was sincerely converted as a young man in Plymouth and in 1826/7 offered to CMS as a missionary for India. The committee asked him if he would consider going to Persia instead, and he agreed. His conception of churchmanship, however, made it impossible for CMS to accept him when it was discovered that he viewed it as right for a layman to celebrate Holy Communion when no clergyman was present.

In 1828 a fortunate legacy of £10,000 enabled him, his wife and two children, his sister and a young deaf man named John Kitto (whom he had rescued from the workhouse as a child and educated) to set off for Baghdad, which they considered a good centre for the evangelisation of Persia. In 1829 they sailed on Lord Congleton's yacht to Copenhagen – and from there made their way to St Petersburg. They then pressed on to link up with the missionaries in the Caucasus and found Dr Glen busy at his translation. Eventually they reached Shusha, where Pfander, always ready for an adventurous journey, agreed to accompany them to Baghdad. At Tabriz, one lady of the party got married and stayed behind. The others pushed on and narrowly escaped being involved in a clash between government forces and rebellious Kurds near Sulaimaniah. Eventually they reached Baghdad in December 1829 and settled down to learn Persian and Arabic and to get to know the people – Jews, Armenians and Muslims. In 1831 Baghdad suffered the worst epidemic of the plague for many years; as a result Mrs Groves and one other member of the party died. Later in the same year the town was besieged by the Pasha of Mosul and the missionaries were in danger of their lives. This seems to have been too much for some of them and John Kitto and Francis Newman, the brother of the Cardinal, who had joined the party in 1830, left for England travelling through Persia together as far as Tabriz. No more is known of this strange episode in the life of the Cardinal's brother, who was subsequently to become a noted secularist and co-founder of University College, London. Groves himself left Baghdad in 1833 and made his way to India where he subsequently did valuable work as an independent missionary in Tinnevelly for a number of years.

Chapter Nine

THE COMING OF THE AMERICANS,
1834-1870

The wave of religious enthusiasm in England, which led among many other things to the founding of the Church Missionary Society in 1799, was also felt in America. A similar interest in missions was aroused there and in 1810 the interdenominational American Board of Commissioners for Foreign Missions was founded. Before long they had a considerable number of missionaries located in many countries round the Mediterranean, including Turkey. The decision to extend their work to Persia seems to have stemmed from a report on the Nestorians by the British chaplain in Constantinople, Robert Walsh. This report was printed in *The Missionary Herald* in 1826. Walsh in turn probably received his information from the traveller, Claudius James Rich.

As a result of Walsh's article, in the spring of 1831 two American Board missionaries working in Turkey were sent to investigate the position in Persia. The report which the two men, the Reverend Eli Smith and the Reverend H. G. O. Dwight, sent to the Prudential Committee of the Board was on the whole optimistic. The Nestorians, they found, existed in considerable numbers, about 125,000 was the estimate; they were poor and illiterate, but they were undoubtedly Christians, and what was even more important they differed in many important respects from the Dominican Roman Catholics, who were already at work in the area. They soon acquired the name 'The Protestants of the East' and as such were, as the report said, 'in imminent danger of being led astray by the ever-watchful, wily and active missionaries of Rome'.

When Dwight and Smith reached Urmiah (in north-western Persia and now renamed Rezaiah), the centre of the Nestorians of the plain, they found it recovering from a serious cholera epidemic which had reduced the population by nearly 50 per cent. They were thus compelled to recognise the health hazards for

102

missionaries, but they were also made keenly conscious of the good that could be done by a medical missionary. All in all, here was a very favourable mission field. They saw the revival of the ancient Nestorian Church as an essential preliminary to the eventual evangelisation of the Muslim population. Revival was their aim; it was not the intention of the founders of the mission to found a new Church but rather 'to enable the Nestorian Church through the grace of God to exert a commanding influence in the regeneration of Asia'.

The first couple to reach the mission field were the Reverend Justin and Mrs Perkins, who reached Tabriz in August 1834. Justin Perkins, the founder of the Persia Mission, was 29 when he reached Tabriz. He was born in 1805 in Holyoake, Massachusetts, the descendant of a certain John Perkins who had come to Massachusetts from England in 1631. He spent his early years on a farm. He studied at Westfield Academy and graduated with honours from Amherst College in 1829. He then had two years as a student at Andover Theological Seminary and was ordained in 1833. He was a remarkable man in many ways; he was a great scholar and linguist and became a member of the American Oriental Society to whose journal he contributed a number of papers; he was also a member of the *Deutsche Morgenländische Gesellschaft*. During his time in Persia he collected a number of valuable Syriac manuscripts which are now in various American and European libraries. He was a man of robust constitution and thanks to his early years on a farm was able to turn his hand to every practical chore. In addition he was a relentless disciplinarian of himself and worked to an unvarying timetable which filled every moment of every day.

When Mr and Mrs Perkins arrived in Tabriz they were greeted by members of the British Embassy who had rented a house for them and who soon became their close friends. In 1835 the British Minister, Sir Henry Ellis, suggested that the American missionaries should ask for British protection. This they did and were officially under British protection until the British diplomats withdrew in 1839. The Americans then sought the help of the Russian Consul-General in Tabriz under whose care they remained until 1851 when they again asked for and obtained British protection which lasted until the first American Minister, Benjamin, was appointed in 1883.

His appointment at this time was due to pressure in Congress for support to be given to the American missionaries.

In 1834 Tabriz was the most important city in Iran and the location of all the foreign Embassies. It was still a walled city and the walls with their eight gates were still in a reasonably good state of repair. It was an important commercial centre for the exchange of goods between Iran and Europe; it is said to have had a population at this time of about 80,000.

In October of that year Perkins, accompanied by the Basel missionary, Haas, made a preliminary reconnaissance to Urmiah. At Galavan they met a Nestorian bishop, who agreed to become Perkins's language teacher. They also paid a call on the Nestorian Patriarch who received them in a friendly manner. Perkins spent the next year ministering to the English-speaking community in Tabriz and in language study, for which he proved to have an exceptional ability.

The need for a medical recruit to join Perkins was very great; at their annual meeting in Utica, New York, in 1834 the Board made an urgent appeal for a doctor to join Perkins. In the audience was a young doctor who had been practising in the town for some years, Dr Asahel Grant. He offered and was accepted and in October 1835 he and his young wife joined Mr and Mrs Perkins in Tabriz. Within a month of his arrival Grant visited Urmiah, where he met the governor, who was delighted to welcome a medical man to the town and found houses for the mission. In November the two couples moved to Urmiah, which was to be the centre of the mission for almost the next 100 years. Two years later two more couples joined them, Mr and Mrs Holladay and Mr and Mrs Stocking. In 1839 the Willard Jones came and in 1840 Dr Austin Wright and with him a Mr Edward Breath, who was a printer.

Perkins, at the end of his book *A Residence of Eight Years in Persia*, describes the mission as it was about this time :

> Our mission premises embrace about an acre pleasantly shaded by numerous tall sycamores, enclosed on all sides by a high mud-wall and entered by a single gate. Within the enclosure are the dwellings of the missionaries (four families), our seminary of about fifty pupils – our girls' boarding school of between twenty and thirty – our printing establishment – in all about 100 individuals, besides our school for young Muhammedans, and our medical dispensary.

The main outlines of the work were thus early laid down on the classic mission-compound pattern. As Perkins wrote in the report just quoted :

> Far away in a benighted land in the heart of a Muhammedan city,
>   We are a garden walled around
>   Chosen and made peculiar ground.
>   A little spot enclosed by grace
>   Out of the world's wild wilderness.

Such isolation and separation was sometimes criticised by later visitors. One, for example, commented adversely on the apparent ease and indeed luxury of the Americans' way of life, instancing the very fine white horse which Perkins always rode. The Roman Catholics, also, were never tired of pointing out how much money the Americans had, claiming that they paid pupils to attend their schools. All this can now be seen in the proper perspective and it seems quite impossible that any other pattern could have been adopted. The Nestorians were so desperately poor, illiterate, and prone to excessive drinking that it was impossible to enter into a relationship of equality with them.

Perkins quickly established a school which was, as a later writer said, 'the first Lancastrian school in Central Asia' (no doubt the monitorial system was essential in view of the shortage of staff). Mr Breath and his printing press soon started turning out pamphlets and Gospel portions and all the missionaries contributed material for printing. But the main work was done by Perkins himself. In 1846 his translation of the New Testament was printed in modern and ancient Syriac in parallel columns, and in 1852 the Old Testament was done in the same way. A periodical called *Rays of Light* was started and before long eighty works had been issued from the press.

Not the least of Perkins's achievements was his work for the Syriac language. He first reduced the spoken language to a systematic form which could be printed. The Syriac used by the Churches was the dialect of Edessa and was scarcely understood by ordinary Christians. The colloquial language was a quite different dialect and not just a debased form of Church Syriac, and it had numerous Persian and Turkish words in it. This was the language used and understood by the great mass of the people. By using it for their translations and for their prayers and hymns Perkins and the other missionaries gave it a standing which has enabled it to become the medium of modern Syriac writing.

Young Doctor Grant was a man of great courage and independent views; he believed, for example, that the Nestorians were the remnants of the lost ten tribes of Israel and wrote a book to prove it. In 1839, finding his health on the plain was bad, he made an adventurous journey to visit the mountain Nestorians, a wild and independent group, whose domain lay partly in Persia and partly in Turkey. They shared the district with the Kurds, who were fanatical Sunni Muslims. The relationship was uneasy, the Kurds were nominally the overlords, but this was reluctantly and only spasmodically accepted by the Nestorians; violence was endemic in the area. Grant spent the winter of 1839–40 with the Nestorians and earned a great reputation as a doctor and became widely respected by both Kurds and Nestorians.

Unfortunately his visit followed closely on the visit to the Nestorians of two other foreigners: W. F. Ainsworth, who had been geologist and surgeon on the British Euphrates Valley Expedition, and H. Rassam, a Chaldean from Mosul, who had served as interpreter to the Expedition. When the Expedition returned to England in 1837 'a strong desire was excited among many to become acquainted with the actual condition of the mountaineer Chaldean Christians'. So under the joint auspices of the Royal Geographical Society and the Society for Promoting Christian Knowledge, Ainsworth and Rassam were sent out again to find out what they could. This sudden influx of foreigners alarmed the Kurds, especially as they seemed to be chiefly interested in the Kurds' vassals, the Nestorians. Ainsworth reports that he met a Kurdish leader who accused him and his party of being 'the forerunners of those who come to take this country' – a not unreasonable supposition under the circumstances.

In July 1841 Grant visited the area again. When he left, the Kurdish leader, Nurullah Khan, attacked and burnt the house of the Nestorian Patriarch, the Mar Shimun. In the following year tension between Kurds and Nestorians increased, tension which was not diminished when Grant opened an extensive establishment at Ashitha. His buildings were located in a very prominent site and looked rather like a fortress, a fact which was commented on by Sir Henry Layard when he visited the area. They were known locally as the *qaleh*, or castle, and both the Kurds and the Nestorians drew their own conclusion as to why they had been built. About this time the Kurds had engaged in an unsuccessful skirmish with the Turks and blamed their failure on the non-co-operation of the Nestorians.

In March 1843 yet another envoy arrived from Great Britain; this time it was the representative of the Archbishop of Canterbury, the Reverend G. P. Badger. He had meetings with the Nestorian leaders including the Mar Shimun, and no doubt they told him of the oppressive nature of Kurdish rule. He does not seem to have been fully aware of the delicacy of the situation, and encouraged the Nestorians to hope for assistance, which neither he nor anyone else could have possibly given them. Thus, encouraged by false hopes, the Nestorians' attitude towards the Kurds became more openly hostile and considerable friction developed. Grant refused to intervene to restore the situation. Instead, he proclaimed his neutrality as a Christian and his determination to abstain from politics, in spite of the fact that earlier in this year (1843) he had visited Nurullah Khan who made it clear that the Kurds intended to attack the Nestorians – a fact of which the Mar Shimun must have been aware when he left the area for Mosul.

Soon after this Grant left for Mosul and the Kurds, profiting by his absence, attacked the Nestorians and a terrible massacre ensued. For a time Grant's name and reputation among the Kurds restrained them from worse excesses. But in 1846 the Nestorians rose against the Kurdish governor and about 10,000 of them out of an estimated total of 50,000 were killed. Grant meanwhile had died of typhus in Mosul in 1844 while tending the sick in an epidemic. He was thus spared the knowledge of the tragic results which his well-meant efforts to remain neutral had brought upon the people he loved and served so well. Some writers have tended to *blame* Grant for the situation which arose, but this would seem unfair. His presence, as did the presence of other foreigners, upset the situation and was misunderstood. But he did his heroic best alone; three of the first four people sent to help him by his Board died of typhus and the fourth never reached him. Dr Wright's visit to Bader Khan Bey, the Kurdish leader, in 1846 could not avert the disaster and peace was not restored until 1847 when the Turks finally took the necessary steps to bring both Kurds and mountain Nestorians under closer supervision.

As a result of their disappointed hopes and tragic situation, many of the Nestorians turned against the Americans, and the two brothers of the Mar Shimun who had died in the uprising actively incited the Nestorians of the plains to reject the Americans. The presence of Roman Catholic missionaries at this time did not make the work of the mission any easier, and instead aroused a competitive and bargaining spirit, which was highly undesirable. The presence of all these foreigners upset the delicate balance between Christians and Muslims. The Christians were subjected to harsh sumptuary laws and many other disabilities and if given any encouragement could, and did, indulge in futile gestures of revolt.

The missions of Ainsworth and Rassam and Badger will be discussed further in a later chapter. But another earlier visitor needs mention here. In 1834 the Committee on Foreign Missions of the Episcopal Church in the U.S.A., perhaps in emulation of the American Board, came to the conclusion that 'the indications of Divine Providence were sufficiently plain to justify the sending of a missionary to Persia, Armenia or Georgia'. An enterprising young clergyman, Horatio Southgate, volunteered for the job. He left America in 1836 and arrived in Persia the following year (in his journal entry for 17 July Perkins records his arrival dressed in Persian costume to avoid attack by the Kurds). He stayed some time with the mission and was much impressed by what he saw. He was pleased to note that the mission 'aims not at the overthrow of the Nestorian Church to which its labours are almost exclusively directed. The missionaries do not interfere in the least degree with the religious practices of the Nestorians'. But he voiced his fears about the future, fears which, as they were soon to be realised, are worth recalling here.

They aim only to impart religious knowledge drawn from the word of God and secular learning of a useful character. . . . But we fear that the time will come when this will not be enough; when missionaries among the Eastern Churches must not only abstain from the introduction of schism themselves, but if they do their whole duty must lend their aid to prevent it originating within the bosom of the Churches. . . . They must curb by prudent counsels the ardent spirit of those who may come to the knowledge of the truth as it is in Jesus Christ. They must teach them to reverence their bishops, to abide where they are in the bosom of the Church, to submit whenever they can with a good conscience, to labour quietly to extend the spiritual dominion of

Christ among their brethren and to abstain from bold and hasty denunciations, even of what is wrong' (Southgate, *Narrative of a Tour through Armenia, Kurdistan, Persia and Mesopotamia*, pp. 303–5).

But such counsels of gradualness and moderation were not likely to appeal to the American Board missionaries, many of whom had found their faith in the revivals of the early years of the century and for whom bishops were scarcely people to be given undue respect. In 1846 the schools moved from Urmiah to a village about six miles away named Seir. In the same year they experienced a remarkable wave of revivalist fervour under the leadership of Miss Fidelia Fiske in the girls' school. Miss Fiske had come out in 1844; she was a graduate of Mount Holyoake College and quietly but with great zeal and efficiency had taken up the school work amongst girls which had been started by Dr Grant's wife, who died in 1839. She combined, in a remarkable way, deep spirituality with great practical ability. She was well able to supervise the building of the new school down to the smallest detail, or buy all the stores for the mission family of forty, or make all the plans and preparations for a long and complicated journey. But it was her loving nature that impressed people most. A colleague wrote of her, 'Miss Fiske's power was her lovingness and this was the steady outflow of her daily life'.

The revival was undoubtedly strong amongst the missionaries themselves and amongst their pupils in the schools. But it had the effect of separating them from the mass of the Nestorian Churches and of encouraging the tendencies which Southgate foresaw would be so dangerous. The second generation of missionaries were far less willing than Perkins to leave the Nestorian Church untouched, and inevitably the split widened. But the work went on and was too much in demand to be stopped. By 1841 the mission had opened seventeen schools in sixteen different villages and in 1851 Mr Stocking, superintendent of the schools, reported the existence of forty-five schools with 871 pupils of whom 203 were women. In 1855 the first Protestant congregation was formed and in 1862 the first Presbytery. The missionaries no longer respected the bishops' right to be the sole persons to give ordination and when they had candidates they were ordained by a priest of their own following. As we have seen, the Lazarist Père Darnis came to Urmiah in 1841 and the tension between the two groups of Christians grew so acute that at one stage the Persian government had to intervene and forbid proselytising between the various Christian sects. When in 1842 the Catholic missionaries were sent out of the country there was great rejoicing in the Protestant camp. However, they never really left the country and thanks to the efforts of Cluzel they were soon reinstated. In 1844 Perkins and Stocking went to Tehran to protest at their continued interference.

It is very difficult for us today, in the modern relaxed atmosphere of goodwill and ecumenism, to understand how bitterly these battles were fought and with what intense dislike and suspicion the two Christian bodies viewed one another. The fact that the American missionaries were all strongly pro-British and the Roman Catholic missionaries were French and so politically opposed to Britain was an additional reason for them to mistrust one another. Even the comparatively mild Perkins said:

> We should never . . have dared in our lack of pecuniary means to open half of the schools, which are now flourishing among the Nestorians, had we not been impelled to do it by the presence of an enemy. . . . Protestants and their missionaries need the scourge of Papacy to keep them humble and especially to arouse them from their slumbers and to prompt them to higher and holier devotedness in the Master's service.

A modern Assyrian writer has justly said: 'The members of the Nestorian community who remained loyal to their own Church felt helpless in the face of Catholic and Protestant vigour.' But in spite of all these difficulties the mission was able to do an enormous amount for the spiritual, educational and physical welfare of the Nestorians. Cholera epidemics like that of 1847 were not uncommon and before the coming of the mission hundreds died without any medical care. But, thanks to the devoted work of men like Dr Austin Wright, many hundreds were saved and a whole new attitude to medicine, sanitation and public health began to develop.

Gradually the mission began to extend its work beyond the confines of the Nestorians. As we have seen, from the earliest time and at the request of the governor the mission taught a certain number of Muslim boys. In 1860 the Reverend John H. Shedd was assigned special responsibility for the Armenians and the native evangelists who had been stationed in Tabriz and Salmas for some years before that. In 1869 two workers visited the Armenians in

Hamadan and as a result of this visit it was decided to open a station there. In this year Perkins died and with his going an epoch in the history of the mission came to an end. In 1870 the American Board for Foreign Missions split up and the Presbyterians withdrew from participation in its work. The American Board then became a Congregationalist body and took over the work in Turkey, leaving the Persia Mission to the Presbyterians. In May 1870, in one of its first acts after the new situation had become settled, the Mission asked their home board to change the name of the mission to 'The Mission to Persia.' A new era had begun.

Chapter Ten

CHRISTIANS AND JEWS IN PERSIA: THE CHURCH'S MINISTRY AMONG THE JEWS, 1844-1960

There have been Jews in Persia even longer than there have been Christians, in fact ever since the conquest of the Babylonian Empire by Cyrus in 539 BC. It seems reasonable to assume that the Jews at present remaining in Persia are the lineal descendants of those Jews who remained in the area after the period of the exile was over.

Since that time the Jews, like the Christians, have had the status of a *millet*, or national minority, with certain rights and privileges, but with many crippling disabilities and always liable to persecution, extortion and contempt. Nevertheless the Jews have survived as a racial and religious community and, when conditions permitted, have flourished and even taken prominent positions in the national life. But for the most part their lot has been pretty grim, especially after the adoption of Shia Islam as the prevailing form of Islam in Iran.

Under Nader Shah, who was certainly no orthodox Shia Muslim, the lot of the Jews improved a little. But one of his actions was to have very sad consequences. He settled a colony of Jews in the Holy City of Meshed, where they had hitherto been forbidden to live. In 1839, less than a century later, these Jews were forcibly made to adopt Islam and were known as the *Jadid-al-Islam*. However they secretly maintained their old faith, and the Jewish colonies in Baghdad and elsewhere did all they could to help them. Forcible mass conversions such as this go far to explain the intense hostility of the Jewish leaders to the attempts of Christian missionaries (most of whom were themselves former Jews) to convert Jews, even when the methods adopted were so completely different.

During the nineteenth century Jewish fortunes in Persia were at a very low ebb. As always during times of weak central government, minorities are peculiarly vulnerable and almost entirely at the mercy

112

2. The Sian Fu Stone. The memorial to the Nestorian missionary outreach in China.

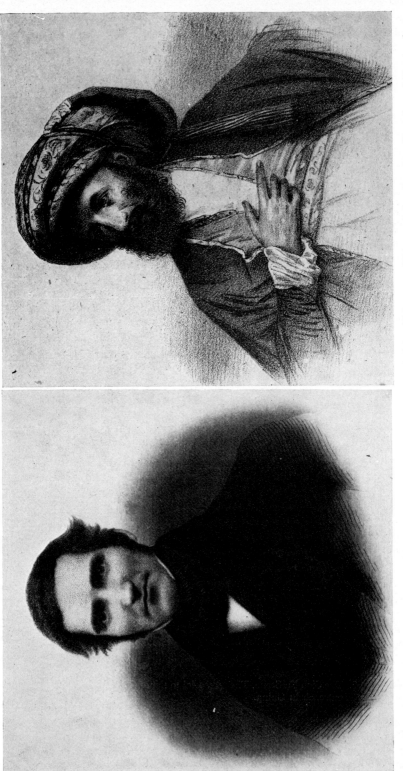

3a. Dr Asahel Grant, the first American missionary doctor.

b. Mar Yohannan, Bishop of the Assyrian Church and the teacher and friend of Justin Perkins.

of local khans and governors. Such was the situation of the Jewish and Christian minorities during the early years of the Qajar dynasty. The Jews being urban and engaged in such despised occupations as the selling of alcohol, the provision of music for weddings, and the peddling of goods to small villages, were more accessible and as a result suffered more than the Christians. Such a small beleaguered community was not likely to be willing to listen to a message which called them out of the security, such as it was, of their own community into the doubtful status of members of another despised community. They did, however, take refuge in some numbers in Bahaism and many looked to the missionaries from the West for political assistance and material help.

We have already given some account of the pioneer missionary to the Jews, Joseph Wolff, and his journeys in Persia between 1824 and 1834. On his return to England Wolff vigorously advocated the establishment of a Christian mission to the Jews in Persia, but it was not until 1844 that such a mission was attempted, and then it was based on Baghdad. In 1844 three men were sent to start a mission in Baghdad, H. A. Stern, Murray Vicars and P. H. Stern-schuss. When they first started up, many Jews flocked to see them, but after a short time the *Chachamim* or Rabbis pronounced a solemn curse on any who set foot in the missionaries' house. This resulted in the virtual cessation of all work for a period of six or seven months. After that they began to trickle back and some even asked for instruction. In the meantime Stern and Sternschuss made two visits to Persia, first visiting Kermanshah and Hamadan, where they distributed considerable quantities of Christian literature and Bible portions and then in November they made a second trip to Basra, Bushire and Shiraz and spent Christmas with the British Resident in Bushire, Samuel Hennell. In Shiraz they found that there were about 350 Jewish families, 25 or 30 of which had become Babis. From Shiraz they proceeded to Isfahan where they spent several months. They suffered a good deal from various minor officials and on one occasion were attacked and robbed. Stern went to Tehran to contact the British envoy, Colonel Sheil, but seems to have felt that he was not given very sympathetic treatment because Sheil was a Roman Catholic. He later paid another visit to Tehran and visited the family of the Shah's doctor, Mirza Nurullah, whose son was to become a leading Christian. From there he went to Hamadan where he sowed the seeds which twenty years later were to result in a Hebrew-Christian community coming into being there. He also visited Kashan and Barforoush. He found many who were Babis and some who remembered Dr Wolff.

Murray Vicars soon left the mission because of bad health and died on the way home. In due course Sternschuss went on leave and the indomitable Stern was left alone. In 1849 he visited the mountain Nestorians, who were beginning to recover from the events of three years previously, but who still lived in daily fear that Kurdish persecution would break out again. Stern stayed with the local bishop who welcomed him as soon as he heard that he was English. He later fell ill and spent some time in the house of C. A. Rassam, who was then British Vice-Consul in Mosul. While he was lying ill in Rassam's house the local Rabbi brought him a large basket of fruit which was then unobtainable in the town. The Rabbi said he had made the journey to a mountain village himself, to get the fruit. Stern was very touched and wrote in his journal: 'I cannot believe he made such a fatiguing tour on my account; still it shows that if a missionary preaches the Gospel in sincerity and truth, without offending the prejudices of those to whom he is sent, he will always enjoy their friendship and esteem' – a fact which many since Stern have found to be true.

In 1852 Stern made another missionary journey in Persia, visiting Kermanshah, Hamadan, Tehran, Barforoush, Damavand and various towns in Mazanderan; but he found conditions so dangerous and the general state of the country so uncertain that he felt compelled to report to his home committee that 'owing to the anarchy then prevailing it was not safe to remain in Persia for long'. For some years after this, the work was carried on from Baghdad, J. H. Brühl and J. M. Eppstein being in charge of the work. Not much was done for Persia beyond the despatch of literature, which found a ready sale amongst the Jews, the Reverend Alexander McCaul's famous book, *The Old Paths: or the Talmud Tested by Scripture*, being very popular.

The presence of permanent foreign diplomatic missions in Persia meant that all kinds of information about the country was becoming available to Europeans. Amongst the information which filtered through was some about the plight of the minorities, both Nestorian and Jewish. The leader of English Jewry, Sir Moses Montefiore, records in his diary that in 1867 he received a report from the British agent, R. T. Thompson, called *Notes on the Jews in*

114

Oormiah, February 1867, which gave chapter and verse for the exceedingly unfair way in which they were subjected to discriminatory taxation and extortions of every kind. As a result of this and of Sir Moses Montefiore's interest, the British government, through their envoy Sir Charles Alison, conveyed a formal protest to the Persian government about its treatment of the Jews.

During the next three years Persia suffered a very bad famine, caused by three years of rain shortage. The famine was made much worse by the failure of the Persian government to control grain hoarders and others who exploited the shortages for their own gain. The situation was so desperate that the British Consul-General in Tabriz informed Sir Moses Montefiore that unless something could be done very quickly for the 300 Jewish families in Shiraz, 'sickness and starvation will shortly annihilate the entire community'. Every major town was affected; in Kazerun 6,000 out of a total population of 10,000 died and in Isfahan conditions were so appalling that 12,000 or more died. It was the situation in Isfahan which made the CMS missionary, Robert Bruce, who had come for a short time to learn the language, decide to stay and do what he could to alleviate the distress, thus eventually giving rise to the foundation of the Church Missionary Society's mission in Persia (see Chapter 13).

In 1871 Sir Henry Rawlinson, the explorer and discoverer of the Behistun inscription, aroused public interest in England and large sums of money were raised for the relief of famine victims. In 1873, when Nasr-ud-din Shah visited England, he was waited on by a deputation from the Jewish Board of Deputies, led by Sir Moses Montefiore, and he promised to give greater care and protection to the Jews in his realm. His statement was lithographed in Hebrew, Persian and English and sent to every synagogue in Persia, where it was displayed inside the main door. There is no doubt that such charitable actions as these disposed the Jews to consider the British, and so also British missionaries, as their friends and as the source of political and material benefits. Throughout the nineteenth century and later, the missionaries did fearlessly espouse the cause of the oppressed and neglected, and did not hesitate to approach their diplomats for assistance on occasion.

Thanks to the extensive itineration of such men as Stern, Brühl and Sternschuss, Christian literature had been widely disseminated in Persia and eagerly accepted by Jews and Muslims. One of the

most remarkable results of this work was the spontaneous formation
of a little group of Jewish-Christian believers in the town of Hamadan. For the most part they were young men of well-to-do Jewish
families known and respected in the town. In 1878 four of them
were baptised by the American missionary, James Bassett, then
stationed in Tehran. Those baptised were Hezkiel Haym, Dr
Rahamin, Dr Moosa and Dr Aga Jan. Two years later their numbers had risen to forty men and fifteen women and they were suffering great persecution at the hands of the Jewish hierarchy, who
even took the desperate step of handing over the converts to the
governor, asking that they should be bastinadoed until they re-
canted. This, as well as imprisonment, payment of heavy fines to
secure release and banning of all Jews from attending Christian
places of worship, caused these fifty-five Christians to appeal to the
CMJ in London; the message was relayed by Dr Bruce. As a result
Joseph Lotka, a Jewish convert from Lemberg and a missionary
of some years' experience, was sent for a three-year tour to Hamadan to see what could be done to sustain and encourage the little
Hebrew-Christian community. In 1883 Brühl was attached to the
Hamadan mission and the two of them besides acting as pastors
to the community in Hamadan also made extensive journeys, visiting
Jews in Gulpayegan and Kashan and many other places. Everywhere they found the Jews to be in a sad and depressed state, often
verging on starvation. Lotka was interested to find that in spite of
their abject poverty many Jewish families had Hebrew New Testaments and that they read them. In 1884 he visited Isfahan where
he stayed with the CMS missionaries and then proceeded to Yezd,
which at that time was an important Jewish centre, there being 400
Jewish families there. He then proceeded to Kerman where he only
found thirty Jewish families and from there he made a dangerous
and difficult journey across the salt desert to Shiraz. In Shiraz he
found a smallpox epidemic raging, but nevertheless he remained
ten days and made contact with the Jewish community, which he
estimated consisted of some 400 families, all of whom were very
poor. He was assisted by the Rabbi in his distribution of Bible
portions – the Rabbi pointing out to him those who could read a
little. From thence he went to Bushire and then by boat to Baghdad.
He did not return to Hamadan, since from 1881 onwards there
had been American Presbyterian missionaries there who undertook
the pastoral care of Jewish Christians. They built what a Jewish

source called 'a synagogue' for them, where much of the Jewish ritual was retained. These Jews remained a separate worshipping group in their 'Peniel' church, as it was called, until 1924 when they merged with the Evangelical Church of today.

In 1888 a young Jewish convert from Tehran, Mirza Nurullah, whose father had been physician to the Shah and whose family was one of the most prominent Jewish families in Tehran, came to England to be trained as a missionary, since he was determined to devote his life to spreading the Gospel of Christ among his own people. After working for a time as a missionary in North Africa he returned in 1889 to work in Tehran where he opened a book depot and reading room and supported himself by giving English lessons, meanwhile holding weekly services in his lodgings. Later that year he moved to Isfahan where he felt he could be more useful.

His arrival coincided with a severe persecution of the Jews who were attacked and stabbed in the streets, their houses plundered and their women molested. The chief *mullah* of Yezd had issued the following proclamation against the Jews which shows how desperate their plight was:

1. No Jew is to wear an aba (Persian cloak).
2. Jews are not to come out of their houses on wet days.
3. Jews are not to touch any article of food in the bazaar.
4. No Jew is to ride any animal through the city.
5. When a Jew dies, any relative who is a convert to Islam may claim all his property.
6. When a Jew buys anything from a Muslim he has to pay 'khoms' (1/5th) to the *mullahs*.
7. All Jews are to wear distinguishing marks on their clothes.
8. When a Jew meets a Muslim, he is to wait for him, salute him and walk behind him.
9. Jews are not to speak in a loud voice to a Muslim.
10. Jews must not eat anything in the presence of a Muslim during the month of fasting.
11. If a Muslim abuses a Jew, the Jew must not return the abuse.
12. No Jew should build a house higher than that of his Muslim neighbours.
13. Muslim merchants must not sell goods to Jewish merchants or pedlars.

117

Of course not all these laws were immediately obeyed, but they provided a loop-hole for dishonest or fanatical people to take advantage of the Jews and to persecute them 'lawfully'. It was during one of these persecutions that Mirza Nurullah sheltered twenty-five Bahais, who were probably converts from Judaism, in his own house, at great personal risk to himself. The civil authority, represented by the Shah's eldest son, the governor of Isfahan, Zillu's-Sultan, was opposed to these laws and eventually had them rescinded. The persecution continued during 1890 and the way was hard for Mirza Nurullah in his contacts with the Jews. Nevertheless he went ahead with his plans and on 20 December opened his little boys' school in Julfa. The opening was attended by the leading Jews and when it was completed the party adjourned to the synagogue where Robert Bruce, the CMS missionary, preached a sermon on the text 'The Messiah Has Come'. The relations between Mirza Nurullah and the English missionaries were very friendly and he used to hold his meetings in Bruce's house.

Mirza Nurullah frequently went on extended journeys, visiting Jews in Kazerun, Bushire and Shiraz, and in all of these places he was invited to speak in the local synagogue. Towards the end of 1891 he was accused of spreading seditious literature and was exiled from Isfahan for six months. He spent the first month of his exile in Kashan and then proceeded to Tehran where he carried on calmly, arranging for the distribution of Christian literature, visiting Jewish communities in the north of Iran, holding services in the American chapel and carrying on extensive commercial correspondence with firms in Europe on behalf of the Jewish merchants of Tehran. This latter activity gained him a great reputation for honesty and helpfulness.

In 1894 he paid another visit to England where he stayed for over a year and carried out a very strenuous programme of speaking. On his return to Tehran he was supported by funds donated by a charitable Irish lady in memory of her son, and he was designated the first 'Charles Eliot Cairnes' missionary. Shortly after his arrival back in Tehran he was joined by Miss M. P. Baily who was to help with work amongst women and children. Miss Baily stayed until 1900 when, on the advice of the Foreign Office, she was recalled as being unsuited to life in Persia and was subsequently relocated to Tunis.

In 1900 another event took place which was to have far-reaching

118

results in the history of the Hebrew-Christian community in Iran: Mirza Nurullah's nephew, Jolinoos Hakim, aged twelve, was baptised. Mirza Jolinoos was to assist and later replace his uncle, and he loyally served the Christian cause in Persia for the next seventy years. A short while previously, in October 1897 to be precise, another figure, who was to play an important part in the building up of the Church, arrived in Tehran, in the form of an able young clergyman, J. R. Garland by name. Garland was due to take up Nurullah's work in Isfahan and in 1898 he started work there. He met with immediate and sustained opposition such as might have broken the spirit of a man less keen on his job. In 1899 a fire destroyed his book depot in Jubareh, the Jewish quarter of Isfahan. Garland thought that the cause was the publication of a pamphlet, *Muhakkal Salaseh: The Truth about the Trinity*, which had caused a great stir. It had been eagerly discussed by the Jews and many were violently opposed to it. Garland promptly took the matter up with Dr Minas Aganoor, the British Vice-Consul, and Preece, the Consul-General, read the Jewish authorities a lecture and demanded that payment for the damage be made. Very soon after he had arrived and had settled the immediate affairs which were waiting for his decision, Garland set out on a journey which was to last fifty-three days. He was accompanied by the mission assistant, Joseph Hakim. Between Najafabad and Khonsar he was accompanied for a while by two Bakhtiari tribesmen, who boasted of the robberies they had committed and the men they had killed, much to the alarm of the servant. However, they did no harm and eventually left the party, who were very thankful to be rid of them. At Gulpayegan, where there had been much persecution, the Jews asked Garland for political help. At Burujerd he preached in English at the synagogue and Hakim interpreted for him. It was here also that he met the great Dr Saeed Khan of Kurdistan, a great Christian, who was at that time physician to the governor of Burujerd. At Koh Rud they fell in with some CMS missionaries, including Bishop Stuart and Garland's own cousin, Dr Latham. He finished his tour by spending two days with Dr and Mrs Carr at Soh, a mountain village about seventy miles from Isfahan where the diocese still has a rest centre.

Garland returned from this trip worn out but extremely happy. There is no doubt that the opportunity presented by missionary work for adventurous journeys such as this were very much appreciated by the missionaries. Garland recorded in his diary that he had worked as hard as a navvy, suffered from extremes of cold and heat and had learnt something about deprivation and hunger, all of which helped him to appreciate the lot of the poor in Persia. The lot of the missionaries themselves was not always easy; Garland had a very unpleasant experience when he was walking alone from the Bank House to Jubareh. He was insulted by a gang of street urchins and when he reacted he was mobbed and spat on and hustled into the presence of Sheikh Muhammad Ali who treated him contemptuously and encouraged his tormentors. He had the melancholy satisfaction of recording the Sheikh's sudden and unexpected death in 1901. In October of this year harassment and persecution of his work and those connected with it was so great that Garland, a man not given to exaggeration, spoke of it as: 'a determined attempt to utterly stamp out the Society's work in Isfahan. Prohibitions have been published in the synagogue; intimidations, threats, blows and bribes have been freely used. . . . I have every reason to believe it is part of a general organised movement against us.' Naturally enough the school attendance dropped, but many pupils still ventured to make the long trek from the Jewish quarter over the bridge into Julfa – many of them starting out very early in the morning in an attempt to avoid their persecutors.

It is hardly surprising that such things should occur since the whole country was in ferment. In 1890, the notorious tobacco concession had been granted to a consortium of Europeans led by an Englishman. It caused such resentment that the religious leaders were able to organise powerful opposition and a ban on smoking, with the result that the concession had to be revoked. From 1900 onwards the unrest grew rapidly, fanned by the innumerable papers which appeared (many abroad), and by the various *anjumans* or secret societies for reform, which were to be found in every city of any size. Much of the opposition was directed against foreigners and so it inevitably brushed off onto the missionaries, especially the British. The demands of the reformers were twofold: firstly, a more democratic form of government with a parliament and elected representatives and, secondly, a more truly national policy which would free Iran from financial exploitation by foreigners. In 1906, after reformers in their thousands had taken sanctuary in the British Embassy grounds in Golhak (Tehran), the Shah very reluctantly granted their request for some form of representative government.

The minorities were to have their representatives in the new parliament and it is a great tribute to Mirza Nurullah's standing with the Jews of Tehran that in 1910 he was asked by them to be their first representative. He declined on conscientious grounds, saying that as a Christian he did not think he could represent them properly – whereupon they asked him to choose someone else for them, which he did.

When the immediate disturbances connected with the constitutional crisis were over, the life and work of the missionaries returned to normal. Garland started a carpentry class in his school, and the pews for the chapel in the new hospital, which was being built by Dr Carr in Isfahan, were made by a convert, Isaac Sassoon. In 1912 another famine struck Isfahan and Garland reported that Jews were reduced to eating husks and grass and that many committed suicide by taking an overdose of opium. The boys' school had celebrated its twenty-first birthday in 1911 and in 1912 a playground was added to it. It had 145 students and the girls' school had 116. The appearance of the Jewish charitable organisation, *L'Alliance Israélite*, drew many children from the school. In Tehran, Jolinoos Hakim, after a layman's course at St Aidan's College, Birkenhead, joined his uncle in Tehran and the schools carried on a precarious existence, being closed for a time in 1911.

The Great War naturally came as a serious interruption to the work of the missionaries; in September 1915 all British subjects were ordered to leave the country. Garland went to Ahwaz but his co-workers Mr and Mrs St Clair Tisdall and their small children left for England and did not return. Garland soon managed to return to Isfahan and during 1916 conditions were less disturbed. He even managed to open a sub-station at Gulpayegan where a school and dispensary were opened under the supervision of Mirza Yussuf Hakim and Mirza Ayub Hakim. Conditions again deteriorated in 1917, when a very serious famine was followed by outbreaks of cholera, typhus and influenza. Many thousands of people died and the missionaries were powerless to do more than relieve the needs of a small number.

After the war the work continued as best it could in Tehran and Isfahan, but Hebrew Christians and teachers in the schools were subjected to a certain amount of persecution and annoyance. With the coming of Reza Khan in 1925, many Jews left the country in order to avoid being drafted into the army. Finally, after a crisis over the inspection of Christian schools by Muslim inspectors and the teaching of the Koran, the Jewish schools in Isfahan were closed in 1928.

In Isfahan, which was the centre of Anglican Church work, an indigenous Church was growing up. In 1927 Garland was appointed Archdeacon by Bishop Linton. As a result, the Hebrew-Christians and the Muslim and Zoroastrian convert Church grew closer together and although the complete diocesanisation of the CMJ work was not to take place for many years to come, there was nevertheless a movement towards an integration of the Jewish Christians into the life of the congregation at St Luke's Church where the other convert Christians worshipped. A similar integration was taking place in Tehran, but owing to the fact that there was no Anglican Church there at that time, the integration of the Jewish Christians was more with the Presbyterians. Mirza Nurullah died in 1925 but his work and name are carried on by his daughter, Gertrude, who after training in England returned as a missionary to Iran and at the time of writing is still living in Tehran.

The schools in Tehran continued to provide an education for the poorer Jewish children who were not catered for elsewhere. In 1928 the numbers were 248 boys and 160 girls. There were also Sunday schools with eight classes and 125 students. All the teachers were Hebrew Christians.

In 1930 the winter was very cold and there were heavy falls of snow. Once more the missionaries were hard put to it to provide the necessary relief. When the thaw eventually came, many houses collapsed, thus increasing the distress. Garland died in 1932, in some respects a lonely and disappointed man, but his work was not without its fruits and his name is warmly remembered amongst many Hebrew Christians of today. He was a shy and scholarly man who always lived alone in Jubareh and devoted his little spare time to transcribing the Bible into Judaeo-Persian. In 1937 the boys' school in Tehran had to be closed – this happened to all minority schools as a matter of national policy.

The Reverend Jolinoos Hakim, who had been ordained in 1935, continued his uncle's practice of frequent itineration and preached in the synagogues of Yezd and Kerman where a number of Hebrew Christians became prominent in the life of the Anglican Church. In 1941 a new crisis hit the schools which had been reopened in Tehran, and once more they had to be closed, this time for conscientious reasons over an unwillingness to teach the Koran in a Christian school. However they were reopened in 1943 along with other schools which were facing a similar dilemma. About this time Miss Nurullah opened an unofficial half-day school for girls which continues up to the present time, in a more orthodox form, providing a useful practical education for girls who are not academically outstanding. During the period since the Second World War a considerable number of Jews have emigrated to Israel, with the result that the total population of Jews in Iran has much diminished. The presence of two Jewish relief organisations has made the educational and charitable work of the Church largely redundant but it still has missionaries engaged in fruitful contact and dialogue with Jews on matters of faith; and of the present Persian clergy, the Reverend Iraj Muttahedeh is Jewish. Since 1968 the work of the CMJ has been fully integrated with the work of the Anglican Diocese of Iran.

Chapter Eleven

THE ARCHBISHOP OF CANTERBURY'S MISSION TO THE ASSYRIAN CHURCH, 1886-1915

Mention has already been made of some of the early English visitors to the mountain Nestorians – Ainsworth and Rassam in 1840 and the Reverend G. P. Badger in 1843. Ainsworth and Rassam's visit, sponsored by the Royal Geographical Society and the Society for the Promotion of Christian Knowledge, was purely exploratory. The report which Ainsworth made to the SPCK prompted the Archbishop of Canterbury and the Bishop of London to look around for someone to send out on a more permanent basis. They chose a young man, then in training at the Church Missionary Society's college in Islington – George Percy Badger of Ipswich, a printer by trade, who had recently been working in Malta with the CMS printing press there. While in Malta he had learnt Maltese and Arabic. Funds were found to support him from the Society for the Propagation of the Gospel and the SPCK again volunteered financial help.

Setting out from England in 1842 Badger and his wife made a leisurely journey eastwards. In Constantinople they met the Reverend Horatio Southgate, whose views on missions to Eastern Christians no doubt influenced Badger. Journeying on, Badger and his wife visited Tokat, where the very same Armenian priest who had buried Martyn nearly thirty years previously showed them Henry Martyn's grave and the tombstone erected by Claudius James Rich. Badger made Mosul his centre of operations and lived with the Rassam family; his sister who was also travelling with them married C. A. Rassam. In March 1843 he visited the mountain Nestorians at Ashitha and saw Grant's impressive school house and mission buildings. His two long talks with the Mar Shimun seem to have been inconclusive and after some days he returned to Mosul. In June he had a letter from the Mar Shimun telling him that the long-expected Kurdish attack had taken place. Grant's buildings had been seized by the Kurds and used as a fortress. Many Christians were slaughtered but some, including the Mar Shimun, escaped to Mosul where they sheltered with Badger.

In April 1844 news reached Badger and his party that the SPG could not see eye to eye with him and was no longer prepared to support him and that he must return to England at once. In 1850 Badger paid another short private visit to the Mar Shimun and in 1852 he published his book, *The Nestorians and Their Rituals*, which is still an important source book for material on their liturgies and was a factor in maintaining interest in them in England. He then accepted a post as a chaplain to the East India Company. When Sir James Outram went to Aden, Badger went with him, and his knowledge of Arabic and his capacity for friendship with the local sheikhs was of great use there. Outram took him with him on the Persian Expedition of 1857 as staff chaplain.

Although they had no direct results, these two visits were sufficient to make the Mar Shimun realise that help might be forthcoming from England, which would act as a counter-balance to the activities of the Americans and the French Roman Catholics. Between 1844 and 1868 various unofficial appeals for help were transmitted to England. In 1868 a more formal appeal for help was made, signed by three bishops, five *maleks* or local chiefs, thirty-two priests and eleven deacons. This appeal seemed sufficiently serious to warrant the sending of yet another mission of inquiry, but it was not until 1876 that the Reverend E. L. Cutts was chosen to be the Church of England representative. He visited the area and wrote an interesting report for the SPCK and also a book of his travels called *Christians Under the Crescent*, published in 1877. It is of interest to us today chiefly because it shows clearly how wide the gap was then between the thinking of the non-conformists and the Established Church of England and how delicate the political aspects of the matter were. Cutts reports certain actions of the American missionaries which seem to him to be unwise : they refuse to accept as members any who are not total abstainers; they refuse to baptise the children of any who are not members; the old missionaries procured the ordination of a new priest from a bishop, the new missionaries procure ordination from one of their own priests. He concludes: 'The Nestorians are strongly attached to their ancient Church. . . . I think it is therefore easy to understand why many of those who were pupils of the earlier American missionaries are

alienated from their successors. . . .' The Americans in their turn
wrote a frank and open letter to the Archbishop of Canterbury.
The points they make are very pertinent. First, they claimed that
their members had been arrested by the Mar Shimun who mal-
treated them and told them that he had made an agreement with
Cutts that none but representatives of the Church of England should
henceforth work in the mountains. Secondly, they rightly point out
the dangers of rivalry: 'we do question the wisdom of planting a
rival mission among a people with so limited a population, a people
of volatile temperament, largely pauperised by unwise benevolence,
and ready to welcome whoever comes with the promise of political
protection, whether Russian, French or English, and especially at a
time when we have to encounter opposition and reproach in our
efforts to counteract the mercenary spirit of the people, and lead
the Churches up to self support and independence.' One cannot help
sympathising with the Americans, who had laboured so hard and
so long in the field. On the other hand the Archbishop's mission
when it eventually came, was to carry on a valuable work parallel
to that of the Americans. Thanks to the tact of the leaders of both
sides, an amicable, if not completely accepting, attitude was to be
found between the Anglicans and the Presbyterians.

The first effort of the Archbishop's mission to implement its
promise to help the Mar Shimun was not a success. In 1881 the
Reverend Rudolph Wahl was sent out to start schools and to help
generally in the education of the Nestorians. He was an Austrian
national and was a priest of the American Episcopal Church. He
did what he could with the limited resources at his command, but
he was not a tactful person and soon got on the wrong side of
everyone. In 1884, on orders from the governor, he was forcibly
expelled from Urmiah and went to live in Tabriz. The Archbishop
sent out Athelstan Riley, a prominent English layman interested
in the Eastern Churches, and H. P. Chomeley to look into the situation. They succeeded in getting permission for Wahl to return to
Urmiah, but they came to the conclusion that he was not the
right man for the job and he was withdrawn in 1885.

The following year the right men were found to start the mission
on a proper footing: Canon A. J. Maclean of Eton and King's
College, Cambridge, Jeremie Prize-winner and ninth wrangler, and
W. H. Browne who had been a curate at the famous Tractarian
church of St Columba's, Haggerston. Both these men were imbued

with Tractarian ideals and were willing to live a celibate life in a communal house and to accept only £25 per annum for their personal expenses. They settled down in the very primitive mission house in Urmiah, which they had acquired, and started to learn the language. Both proved to be remarkably successful in this and Canon Maclean, who was head of the mission, subsequently became a great Syriac scholar and wrote important works on the vernacular dialects of the area. In 1887 they were joined by the Reverend A. H. Lang and in 1888 by the Reverend A. R. Eddington.

The missionaries soon distinguished themselves by their humble, not to say poor, manner of life and their determination to abide by the rule of the mission that 'all imitation of Western customs and manners are strictly forbidden'. They wore their cassocks and they lived at exactly the same standard and in exactly the same way as the Nestorians around them. They also firmly adhered to their determination to distinguish themselves from the American and the Roman Catholic missions by not doing anything which could possibly be interpreted as proselytising. They contented themselves with starting schools for ordinands and others, and setting up a printing press to print liturgical works. Nevertheless, they were English and could not escape altogether from that fact which, in part at least, accounted for the welcome which they received from the Assyrians, of whom Riley rightly wrote: 'there is no doubt that besides the desire for religious aid, the hope of temporal succour and protection enters largely into their calculations.'

In November 1887 the team split up; Maclean and Lang remained in Urmiah and Browne was sent to the Tyari district in Turkey. At the urgent request of the Mar Shimun he made Kochanes his headquarters for the winter, living in a house attached to that of the Mar Shimun and his family, with whom Browne very soon became on terms of closest friendship. The Mar Shimun had told Browne that he feared an attack by the Kurds. When these fears seemed likely to be realised, Browne smuggled a message through to Maclean who alerted the diplomatic authorities in Tabriz and they publicised their knowledge sufficiently to deter the Kurds for a while. Ever since the advent of Abdul Hamid to the Sultanate of Turkey in 1878, the Kurds had been increasingly adventurous and in 1880 had actually crossed the Persian border and tried to use the Persian Kurds to attempt to establish an independent Kurdistan.

Browne was to spend the rest of his life in the Tyari area either at Kochanes, the headquarters of the Mar Shimun, or at Lizan. He soon adopted the habits and customs of the mountain Nestorians and lived exactly as they did, eating and sleeping on the floor and dressing as one of their priests would have done. Riley, who visited him in 1888, has left us a vivid picture of him:

> A thin spare figure stood before me, clad in a double-breasted English cassock, which once was black, but now, discoloured by travel and weather, turned a rusty green. A high conical hat of black felt, round the bottom of which was twisted a black turban covered his head. The face beneath the turban was rather pinched and his hair descended to his shoulders. On his feet were sandals or shoes of rope . . . and in his hand a staff with a crooked head. . . .

This willingness on the part of Browne and the other missionaries to live as the Nestorians did themselves contrasted strongly with the Westernising tendencies of the American missionaries. The Englishmen in their cassocks were more in keeping with Nestorian ideas of a priest than were the American pastors in their frock coats and shovel hats. When Maclean opened schools he was very reluctant to teach the boys English, and he insisted that they should retain their usual habits of eating and sleeping and not be led to believe that Western ways were better.

The educational work expanded rapidly and by 1888 the mission was responsible for high schools in Urmiah, Superghan and Ardishai and forty village schools, of which seventeen were in Turkey and the remainder in Persia. They had a total of 1,200 scholars in these schools and used a considerable number of Assyrian clergy to teach in them. Their other main work was the preparation of works for the printing press, especially service books. Previously each church had had its own manuscript service book. These varied considerably, some containing more than others. Maclean, by collating a large number of these manuscripts, was able to produce and print a service book more complete than any manuscript one. When these were distributed they were much appreciated. As time went on they also printed Bible portions and commentaries, a catechism which every scholar had to learn, school books and a Persian-Assyrian grammar for those Nestorians who could not speak or read Persian. In all, over thirty works were issued from the printing press, many of them being real contributions to scholarship.

In 1890, four members of a small Anglican order of nuns, the Sisters of Bethany, of Lloyd Square, London, came out and started educational work amongst women and children. Their work was greatly appreciated and amongst their pupils they had Surmia, niece of the Patriarch of the time and sister of the murdered Patriarch Benjamin, whose place she took on his death at the hands of the Kurds.

But the resources of the mission were very limited and, contrasted with the numbers and wealth of the American mission, must have seemed very inadequate. The total income of the Archbishop's mission in 1887 was £1,300 compared with about $25,000 (= £5,500) for the Americans. Maclean resigned from the mission in 1891 on being appointed Bishop of Moray in Scotland, but he continued to take a keen interest in its work. The Sisters of Bethany had all retired by 1900 and from then on the mission rarely consisted of more than four or five members.

The presence of a number of apparently wealthy foreigners suggested the idea to certain enterprising but somewhat unscrupulous Assyrians that there might be easy money to be obtained from benevolent Christians in Europe and America. Numerous unofficial envoys went abroad and solicited funds for famine relief, for schools, colleges and orphanages, and collected considerable sums of money – very little of which was used for the purposes for which it was intended. Canon Maclean and others issued repeated warnings against such persons, but they went on going, and receiving.

There is no doubt that these isolated and persecuted Christians caught the imagination of many missionary-minded people in Europe and America. Some of the more reliable self-sent envoys were able to persuade a society to support them. About 1880 an Assyrian from Wazirabad named Pera Johannes went to Hermansberg in Germany and was ordained as a Lutheran priest. He returned to his native village and in due course built a church. In 1905 he was joined by his son, Luther Pera Johannes, who had also been trained in Germany. From 1893–5, N. G. Malech was supported by a Norwegian group called the Evangelical Lutheran Mission. When they could no longer find the money to support him, Malech went to America where he founded the Persian Christian Benevolent Society of Chicago, most of whose officers seem to have been expatriate Assyrians like himself. About 1896 the Germans opened three orphanages, in Khoi, Sobujbulak and Delgusha. John Joseph lists the following societies which were working among the Nestorians at the turn of the century : the United Lutheran Church of America; the Evangelical Association for the Advancement of the Nestorian Church; the German Orient Mission; Plymouth Brethren from England; Dunkards; Holiness Methodists; Southern Baptists; Northern Baptists; and English Congregationalists. He concludes with what all must surely agree are hard but just words :

> There was perhaps no missionary field in the world where there were so many rival 'Christian' forces at work, as were found in Urmiah at the beginning of this century, all struggling to get prominence among these few people. Some of the results of this unseemly struggle were demoralisation and arrogance on the part of Persian Christians, the transformation of religion into a sport and a trade. These factors lowered Muslim respect for the Christian community and increased their jealous resentment of the self-assertiveness as well as the prosperity of their neighbours (Joseph, *The Nestorians and their Muslim Neighbours, p.* 123).

The danger of this kind of competition is not yet over, as a glance at the list of Sunday services offered in Tehran in the English language newspapers would indicate.

The above-described state of affairs may have been one of the reasons why the Archbishop's mission decided in 1903 to move the centre of its work from Urmiah in Persia to somewhere in Turkey. The old Mar Shimun died in this year and was replaced by his nephew Benjamin. His home, Kochanes, was in Turkey as were numerous other important centres of Christian population. W. A. Wigram, who joined the mission in 1902, was located at Van where there was a British Consul. It was for this reason that the mission first decided to make Van their new headquarters, but later on for geographical reasons they chose Amadia.

The situation of the Nestorians and the Kurds remained extremely tense and there were frequent outbursts of fighting. In 1896 a prominent Nestorian bishop, Mar Gauriel, had been murdered by the Kurds and his murderers had never been brought to justice. In 1900 Kurds attacked one of the German orphanages and carried off some of the children. In 1902 Browne reported from Tyari that the Kurds were very aggressive that year and that trouble was brewing. In 1908 5,000 Kurds invaded the Tyari district and sacked and burnt all but 3 of the 500 houses there.

In 1910 Browne died as the result of a fall, which aggravated a long-standing chest condition. He died in Kochanes on Holy Cross day and was buried in the little church there, as he would have wished. With his death the last links with the heroic beginnings of the mission were broken. He had served for twenty-four years, during which time he took only two leaves in England. He was replaced by the Reverend G. J. McGillivray, who frankly admitted that he could not accept the primitive conditions and austerity which Browne had accepted; an epoch was at an end.

Wigram retired in 1911 after giving ten years of devoted service to the Mission. Before he did so, virtually all the mission work had been transferred to Amadia. Only the American Neesan was left in Urmiah where he ran a small school for 'boy-bishops', i.e. the nephews of bishops who might expect to take their uncles' place in due course. In 1912 Neesan was joined by the Reverend O. F. Spearing, the last recruit to the mission.

When war broke out in 1914 the Turks crossed the Persian frontier almost immediately and fighting between the Turks and the Russians broke out all around Urmiah. McGillivray and Reed got away in November 1914 but Spearing, Barnard and Neesan remained. When the Russians retreated in January 1915, Spearing and Barnard, being members of a combatant nation, thought they had better leave too. They arrived at Tabriz with Cordonnier, the Belgian customs chief. When they got there they found the city expecting to be taken at any moment by the Turks. So they commandeered a carriage and drove on to Julfa; from there they went to Tiflis and so got home via Petrograd, Finland and Norway, where they caught a boat from Bergen to England.

The mission was never reopened. Maclean eventually became Primus of Scotland and died in 1943 aged 85. Wigram vigorously espoused the cause of the Assyrians after the war and wrote and spoke on behalf of the survivors. His pamphlet, *Our Smallest Ally: A Brief Account of the Syrian Nation in the Great War,* was published in 1920 and his work on *The Assyrian Settlement* in 1922. But fortune did not favour the survivors. Like the Kurds, their traditional enemies, they were a nation without a homeland. Many emigrated to America, a number stayed on in Iraq, and some returned to their ancestral home in Persia. Wigram eventually

131

became a canon of St Paul's in Malta and in the inter-war years became a well-known lecturer for the Hellenic Travellers' Club cruises. The other members of the mission dispersed to various jobs and the work was at an end. Perhaps its most lasting memorial is enshrined in the hearts of those who were educated in a mission school : it is selfless men like Maclean, Browne and Wigram who are still remembered with affection by Assyrians in Persia and elsewhere.

Chapter Twelve

THE PRESBYTERIAN MISSION TO PERSIA

1870 – 1934

Soon after the Presbyterian mission took over in Persia in 1870, one of the missionaries clearly described their current attitude towards the Assyrian Church: 'The old Church is a fossil,' he wrote, 'it is the grave of piety and Christian effort. It can never be reformed. Hence for our Christians to live at all, they have been compelled to leave it . . . the separation is complete.' It seems sad now that this separation should have come about; the pioneer missionaries never intended it. But in view of the enormous gulf in religious attitudes, culture and standards of living between the missionaries and the Nestorians, it seems to have been inevitable.

So in 1870, when the process of separation was complete, it was natural that the missionaries should look for wider fields of activity and consider work amongst the Armenians and the Muslims. This too was not an entirely new idea, but was the culmination of a movement of expansion that had been going on for some time.

TEHRAN

The first new work to be undertaken was in Tehran. In 1872 the Reverend James Bassett came out and, after considering the rival claims of Hamadan and Tehran as suitable places for a new mission station, decided on Tehran. In November 1872 he took up residence there with his wife and family. His choice was a wise one, for Tehran, although it had not the historical associations of Tabriz, Isfahan or Shiraz, was the Qajar capital. It was much smaller then than it is today – its population was only 60,000 with about 110 Armenian and 300 Jewish families and a very small number of Zoroastrians.

Bassett wisely decided to make Persian the language of his mission, in spite of the fact that most of his early contacts were with Armenians. By 1876 there were enough converts to warrant the founding of a church, whose services were sometimes attended by Muslims. In 1880 a government order forbade Muslims to attend services and the chapel was closed. But services were resumed in 1882 and, from then on, all who wished were free to attend. By then Bassett reported that the church had twenty-nine members and that recent converts included four Muslims, one Jew and three Armenians. In 1883 a new chapel was built on land near the Shemiran Gate, in spite of intrigues on the part of the Shah's chamberlain, Aminu's-Sultan, who later became Prime Minister. Bassett carried on all the activities of the mission – teaching, preaching and translating. He was a good Persian scholar and was in contact with Robert Bruce of Isfahan and collaborated with him on the translation of the Bible. There was even talk of the Presbyterians taking over the Julfa station if the CMS were unable to do so. In 1876 he compiled the first hymn book which was printed at a Muslim press in Tehran. In 1878 he obtained his own printing press and began producing Christian literature, including his own translation of *Pilgrim's Progress*.

Educational Work

The earliest schools which Bassett started were attended solely by Armenians and met with some opposition from the ecclesiastical authorities. In 1887 the Reverend Samuel Ward and his family joined Bassett and opened a boarding department for the school. Ten years later this school was handed over to Mirza Nurullah of the London Jews Society (see p. 118).

1896 will always be remembered by Christians in Iran as the year when Dr and Mrs Jordan arrived from America. Jordan was undoubtedly the greatest missionary educator ever to work in Iran. Under his guidance a new school was started and it rapidly expanded until by 1901 it had all the classes necessary for a complete high school. In 1913 a new site was purchased outside the city. During the war, two residences and a boarding department were built. In 1924 the main buildings were added so that by 1933 the campus occupied some forty-four acres. This was the famous Alborz College, which, with the Stuart Memorial College in the south, had a virtual monopoly of modern education in Iran for the first thirty years of this century.

These were schools for boys, but the work for girls was not neglected. In 1874 a small day school was opened with twelve pupils. A year later it moved to more commodious premises in the Lalezar area. The early pupils were accepted on a contract basis, free of all charge, the parents agreeing to leave the children in school for a set number of years. By 1883 fees were gradually being introduced and the contract system was abandoned in 1888. In 1884 the school moved yet again, this time to the newly-purchased mission compound in Qavamu's Sultaneh and was known as Iran Bethel, under which name it had a long and honourable career. Little by little, Muslim girls began attending these schools in such numbers that in 1903 the Shah issued an order directing all parents to remove their daughters from the school as 'they were being taught to wear high shoes and long skirts'.

Medical Work
Medical work was obviously a desirable line for missionary work in Tehran, so when Bassett returned from his first leave in 1881 he was accompanied by Dr W. W. Torrance, who was joined seven years later by the first woman doctor ever to be seen in the capital, Dr Mary Smith. Persian medicine at this time was very primitive, so the court, the aristocracy and anyone else who could afford it patronised foreign physicians, who often became very influential. Both the missionary doctors were much in demand, and in 1883 when Persia was sending its first diplomatic representative to the United States, Torrance was given five months' leave of absence to accompany him at the request of the Shah. In 1891 a serious cholera epidemic broke out in the city and the work of the missionaries, who were helped by a group of Persian boys from the mission school, was much appreciated.

For some time the mission had been negotiating to open a hospital and in 1887 had actually got as far as buying a piece of ground on which to build it. But the Shah made such impossible conditions – for example, no women were to be admitted, the call to prayer was to be given daily by a member of the hospital staff – that for some years little progress was made. However in 1893 a new missionary doctor, Dr J. G. Wishard, came and he managed to get these conditions waived and a hospital was built. Wishard made a great impression during his ten years' service and his autobiographical account of his time in Persia makes interesting reading. While he was in Tehran, he worked with the doctors of the Indo-European Telegraph Company in training a group of Persians in modern Western medical methods. In the cholera epidemic of 1904 a pamphlet which he had written was translated and widely circulated in the city, and his organisation of relief and sanitary care became a model for future operations of the same sort.

HAMADAN

In 1879, as we have seen, Bassett paid a visit to Hamadan and baptised a number of Jews, but permanent work did not start until the arrival of the Reverend J. W. Hawkes in 1881. His early years in the town were extremely chequered owing to the opposition of Jewish authorities. Jewish converts were arrested, fined and persecuted, and on one occasion Hawkes himself was arrested. Hawkes stayed in Hamadan for fifty-two years; as far as can be ascertained this is a record for missionary service in Iran. During that time he saw many changes for the better and the church and mission were not long in becoming an accepted part of the life of the town. Hawkes, like Bassett, was a good Persian scholar and he assisted in the translation of the Bible and also produced the first *Qamus*, or Bible dictionary, which was much in demand amongst Persian scholars.

Educational Work

In 1870 two Armenian evangelists had started a small school among the small Armenian colony in Hamadan. Hawkes took over this work and when asked by the Jewish Christians to start a school in the Jewish quarter he transferred the school there. In 1882 Miss Annie Montgomery came out and started work amongst girls. Three years later, thanks to the generosity of Miss Faith Hubbard and Mrs Sherwood (the mother of Mrs Hawkes), a fine new building was erected which became known as the Faith Hubbard School.

Medical Work

A year after he arrived Hawkes was joined by Dr E. W. Alexander, who began the medical work in the town. In 1892 Alexander was replaced by Dr George W. Holmes, who became personal physician to the Shah and during his many years in Persia was very much respected as a physician and medical educationist. On the arrival of Dr Blanche Wilson Stead in 1900 hospital work was started in a very small way, and under the guidance of Dr Arthur Funk it grew and developed. A large hospital was soon built and in 1927 a women's department was opened.

TABRIZ

Tabriz was opened as a sub-station of Urmiah in 1873, when Mr Coan, Mr and Mrs Easton and Miss Jewett were located there. At first they concentrated on the numerous Armenians in the town, and as usual they met with some opposition. However, they soon found that their meetings were also being attended by Muslims. They carried out a lot of village evangelism and as a result of a visit to Khoi a certain Mirza Ibrahim was converted. He became so brave in his witness that he had to leave his native town and go to Urmiah where he was employed as an itinerant evangelist at a salary of four dollars a month. Once more his fearless preaching got him into trouble. He was arrested and sent to prison in Tabriz. After nearly a year he died of injuries inflicted by his gaolers and fellow-prisoners who tried to make him recant. In 1899 the success of the mission was deemed sufficient to warrant the building of a small church.

Educational Work

Teaching had, as usual, been one of the earliest and most welcome occupations of the missionaries. Miss Jewett opened a girls' school in 1879, and from 1899 to 1924 this work was carried on with great success by Miss Lily Beaber. With the arrival of the Reverend S. G. Wilson in 1880 a boys' school was started and was carried on by him until his death in 1916.

Medical Work

Medical work in Tabriz was started in 1881 by Dr George W. Holmes. He was joined by Dr Mary Bradford in 1888 and in 1890 Dr William Vanneman came out and served faithfully there for the next forty years, building up a great reputation in the town and for many miles around. In 1893 a hospital was built and soon afterwards nurses' training was begun. Dr Alexander's (see p. 136) chief claim to fame is, perhaps, that he trained the famous Dr Saeed

Khan Kurdistani and gave him his first chance of becoming a doctor.

Saeed Khan was one of two sons of a *mullah* who were orphaned at an early age. Saeed was a brilliant scholar and being the son of a *mullah* was exceptionally well versed in Muslim theology – very early in life he was admitted to the local branch of the Nakhshbandi sect of Sufis. In 1879 two Bible Society colporteurs and a Protestant Assyrian pastor, Kasha Yohannan, visited Senneh (the home town of Saeed Khan). Previously he had had some contact with a group of Chaldaean Christians in the town but this was his first real contact with Christians keen on evangelism. The two colporteurs sold him a New Testament and discussed his problems with him, and on leaving introduced him to Pastor Yohannan. They exchanged lessons in Syriac and Arabic, and Saeed soon became convinced that he was in fact a Christian. He announced this to his brother Kaka, who was horrified. The news spread through the town and the boy's life was in danger so he fled to Hamadan. Here he contacted the Christians and, after a short spell looking after Dr Alexander's horses, his capabilities were recognised and he was employed as a teacher in the Faith Hubbard School. He fell in love with a fellow teacher, the daughter of an Assyrian pastor. News of their impending marriage caused such anger amongst the Muslim inhabitants that there was a riot and the governor was concerned for public safety. However the matter was dropped when the crowd was told that Saeed Khan was a Kurd and so a Sunni Muslim and not a member of the prevailing Shia sect.

Saeed Khan learnt all he could from Dr Alexander and then went to England for further training. Eventually he became one of the most qualified Persian doctors of the time and was for several years the personal physician of Ain-ed Dowleh, a relative of the Shah. All who met him were deeply impressed by his simple Christian faith, which he never attempted to conceal. His subsequent life until his death in 1942 was one of uninterrupted service and Christian witness of a kind that makes him one of Persia's outstanding Christians.

MESHED

In 1894 the Reverend L. F. Esselstyn visited Meshed, the holy city of Shia pilgrimage in north-eastern Persia. After that he visited many other places in the area, but it was not until 1911 that he was formally permitted to take up residence and open a mission station in Meshed. For the first four years he was there alone, but in 1915 he was joined by Dr Joseph Cook and later Dr Hoffman and medical work was started. By 1917 the situation in the city was desperate and Esselstyn undertook relief work, raising considerable sums of money from wealthy Persians and the foreign community. The hospital buildings were turned into a soup kitchen and eventually nearly a thousand people were being fed every day. In 1918 typhus broke out in the city and Esselstyn, who had never spared himself and was worn out by his efforts, caught the disease and died.

Up to his death very few Persians had been baptised, but after the war a new hospital was built (1923) and some residences. Drs Hoffman and Lichtwardt worked there, the latter undertaking work amongst lepers. The station was never a big one – in 1935 the staff numbered only eleven.

RESHT

Work in Resht was started in 1902 with the arrival of Dr and Mrs Schuler. Previously it had been visited from Tehran. In 1905 the governor of the town gave Dr J. D. Frame the chance of a government hospital, but this arrangement did not prove satisfactory and soon afterwards a mission hospital with thirty-one beds was opened. The work was continued until the outbreak of the First World War and then stopped for the duration. In 1918 the hospital reopened and carried out relief work amongst the famine-stricken inhabitants of the area. In 1921 the district was invaded by the Russians who took over the hospital buildings. Resht was a very unhealthy place and the early missionaries in particular found the climate very trying. There were few converts but a small church was established and educational work was carried on for a time.

KERMANSHAH

As was the case with many other mission stations, the work in Kermanshah was started by native evangelists. In 1894 two of them organised a small school and carried on educational and evangelistic work, being supported by visits from Hamadan and elsewhere. Among those who visited were Mr and Mrs Stead. In 1905 the Steads took up permanent residence there and in 1907 Mrs Stead (who was a doctor) added a few rooms on to her dispensary and began to accept in-patients. They continued in this unofficial way until 1911 when the work was officially recognised and Kermanshah was made a mission station.

During the war the Steads found themselves ministering to the various armies, fugitives and displaced persons who flooded into the town – Russians, Turks and English as well as Assyrians, Armenians and Persians. After the war the Church received generous help from the United States, particularly from the Westminster Church in Buffalo, and the hospital was very well restored and equipped.

As a result of the war there were many orphans and the Steads felt that they ought to do something for them. They started an industrial farm school at a village called Faraman, about seventeen miles from Kermanshah. The work demanded considerable resources and in 1925 the mission felt that they could no longer be responsible for it. The Steads continued on an independent basis and the work was well supported by contributions from America and later was assisted by personnel from the interdenominational International Mission.

Two events during the period under review had an immense effect on the various mission stations. The first was the constitutional crisis and the Russian invasion of North Persia, during the period 1900–12. The extremely unsettled state of the country at this time made the work of the missionaries in Urmiah and the surrounding plain very difficult and disrupted many of their congregations. Many Assyrians fled to Russia and a Russian priest who lived in Urmiah was the centre of much trouble and disaffection, being more concerned with politics than religion. In Tabriz, also, the missionaries were much concerned as the town was a centre of the Nationalist movement fighting for the restoration of the Constitution. In 1909 a locally-employed teacher at the mission school, Howard Baskerville, a graduate of Princeton, became very interested in the Nationalist movement, which he ardently supported. In April of that year he resigned his position as a teacher and devoted himself full-time to the Nationalist cause, training their volunteers. Later in the same year he and an English journalist were killed while fighting to keep open a route for supplies to reach the starving city.

Although not a missionary – in fact, the missionaries at the time were rather embarrassed by his lack of neutrality – Baskerville is remembered today as an example of the American's love of liberty and opposition to all forms of tyranny. On the fiftieth anniversary of his death ceremonies were held in the Iran America Society in Isfahan and doubtless elsewhere.

Very soon after the settlement of the constitutional crisis the country was again upset by the outbreak of the First World War. Once more the whole of the north of the country was thrown into utter confusion. The Russians occupied Urmiah in 1914 but at the beginning of 1915 withdrew. On 4 January the Turks appeared and soon after them the Kurds, led by Simko. This was the signal for a general exodus: 10,000 Assyrians left with the departing Russians and 3,000 took refuge in the French Catholic mission, while no less than 17,000 crowded into the American mission. John Joseph, in his book *The Nestorians and Their Muslim Neighbours*, has described the achievement of the American missionaries at this time:

> But it was the score of American missionaries here who performed one of the most heroic achievements of the war. They proved to be the real saviours of the Christian Persians and during the long war years fed thousands of starving Kurds and Persian Muslims from their meagre stores . . . the man who carried the chief responsibility during these chaotic days was Dr William A. Shedd, born in Urmiah where his father had been a missionary before him.

With the end of the war it was obvious that the work in Urmiah was almost completely at an end. Late in 1923 the missionaries returned, and the Fiske Seminary for Girls and the American School for Boys were reopened. But in 1934 all foreigners were politely but firmly requested to evacuate Azerbaijan and a century's work was ended. The Church has survived as a small body of about 1,000 Protestants, still faithful and still influential in the councils of the Evangelical Church but only a faint shadow of what they were once.

Other stations were opened at Qazvin, Darband and elsewhere, but permanent work was not founded in any of these places. Such, very briefly, is the history of the early years of the mission's independent work up to the centenary year of 1934.

An important step in the evolution of a national Church was taken in 1933 when the Church was reorganised into three district assemblies with a total membership of 2,272. Each assembly elected five delegates to a general assembly which held its first meeting in Sultanabad in August 1934. At this time the parent body, the Synod of New York, relinquished its control over the Church which was then reconstituted as the independent Evangelical Church of Persia with its own synod or *ittehadieh* and complete freedom from external control.

1935–1960

The second part of this account of the American mission to Persia and the Evangelical Church must, of necessity, be dealt with in more summary fashion. I am much indebted to the article by the Reverend Cady H. Allen in *The Crisis Decade* (mentioned in the bibliography, p. 188), for many of the facts incorporated in this section.

The period covers some of the most momentous years Iran has ever known: the final years of Reza Shah's reign; the outbreak of the Second World War; the invasion of the country by the Allies and the abdication of Reza Shah; the post-war problems of scarcity and rising prices; the oil crisis and the Mussadegh area; and the beginnings of the present happy period of progress and expansion.

1936 saw the Shah's programme of reform and reconstruction in full swing. This was the year of the great unveiling, when all women were compelled to abandon the traditional all-enveloping veil. The wives of government officials were ordered to accompany their husbands to all official fuctions and to wear Western dress, including hats. Missionaries of the time have many stories about how they were able to help these unfortunate wives with hats, dresses and advice on hairstyles, etc. The reverse would more likely to be true today, so quickly have the women of Iran adapted to Western styles of dress. By 1938, when the Shah laid the last rail of the line linking the oilfields area with the Caspian Sea, transport and roads had made great headway. Motor cars were a commonplace and there was a system of inter-city buses, which worked quite well unless, as was not infrequently the case, the driver was an opium addict.

But the shadows of the impending war in Europe were already being cast on Iran. Reza Shah was favourably inclined towards Germany and was convinced that the Germans would be victors in the coming battle. Perhaps it was as a result of this feeling that in 1939, shortly before the outbreak of war, the missions were faced with a peremptory demand to hand over their schools within seven days, since all foreign-owned schools or schools that received funds from abroad were henceforth forbidden. Thanks to top-level diplomatic intervention, a year's grace was given to the missions, but when the time was up the order had to be obeyed.

The order could not have come at a worse time for the mission schools, which both in the north and the south were at the peak of their influence and efficiency. The Alborz College was full and widely admired, and places were coveted by many. Only two years previously the long-planned-for Sage College for Women had been opened, and in the year 1938–9 no less than 2,000 Iranian students were being educated in the Presbyterian mission schools. After months of negotiations, all the properties except the Girls' Middle School in Tehran were sold to the government for $1,200,000 and over a century's educational work was at an end. Subsequent endeavours in the field of education, such as the recently opened Damavand Ladies' College, are on a very different basis.

Perhaps it would not be inappropriate here to quote the words of an Iranian historian and social scientist, Dr Mehdi Heravi, which sum up his view of the effect of the American missionaries' work in a way which seems fair and reasonable :

The most important shift in the orientation of Iranian thinking was not brought about by the American government, but by the American Presbyterian mission. These missionaries contributed significantly to Iranian life. If one were to measure this effort on the part of the American missionaries solely by the number of conversions made from Islam to Christianity, it would have to be considered a failure. However, the impact of the missions' work was humanitarian and was strongly felt in the fields of education, public health, charity work and social change. (Heravi, *Iranian American Diplomacy*, pp. 113–14.)

Not every Persian historian would entirely agree with this analysis, but certainly the vast majority of those who were educated in the mission schools, or trained in the hospitals, or were the recipients of social, medical or charitable attention, would wholeheartedly endorse it.

In Tehran, the one educational institution which continued to function was the Community School, which was originally founded to cater for missionaries' children. The presence of a number of expatriate families in the capital soon compelled the school to accept any children who wanted to be educated on English or American lines. Before long the school was catering for children of no less than twenty different nationalities.

With the closure of so much educational work a number of missionaries resigned, but others stayed on and looked around for new fields of service. Some of the most effective work was done in the field of social service; for example by Miss Jane Doolittle and Mrs Payne who revived the name Iran Bethel and besides giving part-time education to girls, also ran a centre for poor women and their children whom they found to be in desperate need of help. Similar work was done in the slums of south Tehran by the Reverend R. Y. Bucher who started the Clinic of Hope. Here women and children were taught the elements of sewing, reading and writing, and given ante-natal care and post-natal clinical attention. A number of Persian doctors and other helpers gave part-time voluntary assistance to Bucher's work.

At the outbreak of the war there had been fourteen doctors in six hospitals and one out-station dispensary. During the war eight doctors either died or resigned and the medical work underwent a radical change. In 1945–6 there were only three doctors on the field and the recruits never again matched the need. In 1954 the position seemed momentarily to brighten when Hamadan Hospital was opened after four years' closure due to lack of staff, and new hospital buildings were dedicated in Resht. But the writing on the wall was obvious to all in these institutions. Rising costs and lack of medical recruits made it impossible for the hospitals to carry on. Within fifteen years all the hospitals were sold off or transferred to private hands and none remained the property or concern of the mission or Church.

Throughout this period the young independent Church was beset with many problems – some usual for any new and inexperienced organisation struggling to survive, and some peculiar to this particular situation. First and foremost of the Church's problems was the lack of adequate leadership and the almost total

144

4. The Reverend Robert Bruce, founder of the C.M.S. Mission in Persia.

absence of a national pastorate – a problem which has by no means yet been fully solved. The reasons for the lack of national leaders and pastors are many. Among them may be mentioned the lack of security in the life of a pastor and the absence of an adequate pension scheme. The custom of sending ordinands to America for their training resulted in the sad fact that there are more Persian pastors ministering in the United States than there are pastors in Persia.

Besides the leadership problem, though related to it, are the problems connected with the fact that there are three distinct language groups in the Church: the Assyrians and the Armenians of Christian origin and the Persian-speaking converts to Christianity. These diverse backgrounds have made it difficult for the Church to think and act in a united fashion and have made it easy for factional thinking to predominate.

Finally the relations between the mission and the Church have not yet been satisfactorily solved. Questions as to the sincerity of the transfer of real power and authority from the mission to the Church have often been raised, not least by the missionaries themselves. As the mission report of 1949 puts it: 'To a large extent the mission has been calling the tune and beating the time. It would seem that a change in the management of the orchestra is overdue.'

But by no means everything was loss and confusion. Indeed, much useful work continued to be done. The task of primary evangelism was not neglected and the work of a missionary of the old school, the Reverend W. M. Miller, was very important in this field. For besides doing a great deal of basic itinerating evangelism himself, Miller bought a garden in north Tehran and held summer schools there for those who could not spare the time for full-time training. In this 'Garden of Evangelism', over a period of years a very thorough course in evangelism, Bible study and the maintenance of a personal spiritual life was provided. These courses were attended by many from the south and have provided the Church with a backbone of informed lay men and women, who may, in the long run, prove to be more valuable than anything else.

In 1959 the mission had sixty-five full-time missionaries on the field. Since then the numbers have decreased considerably. Those who remain, however, are confident that useful work can still be done and that the Church is growing in independence and spiritual

K

145

maturity and could survive even if all outside help were to be withdrawn. Time alone can show whether this optimism will be put to the test and, if tested, whether it will prove to be well founded. But should the vagaries of history involve the country – and so the Church – in further cataclysmic upheavals like those it has known in the past, we may be certain that the Persian genius will again rise to new heights and that at some date thereafter Christian missionaries will be found ready and willing to come to Iran and devote their lives to planting once again the message of Jesus there.

Chapter Thirteen

THE C.M.S. IN PERSIA
PART I: 1869-1919

The third in order of appearance on the field was the English Church Missionary Society, usually known as the cms, which was the major result (in terms of missionary outreach) of the Evangelical movement of the mid-eighteenth century in England. It numbered among its founders and earliest supporters such men as Wilberforce, Pratt, Grant and Venn, and other members of the so-called Clapham sect. It was founded in 1799 and during the early years of its existence it did not succeed in recruiting missionaries in England for service overseas, but had to turn to the Continent.

This shortage of missionaries during its early years led the Society to spend a good deal of its time and money on the provision of translations of the Bible and tracts and Scripture portions in the various languages of the East. In its first annual report of 1801 it considered the advantages of Chinese as a widely-used language in which to provide Christian literature. In the following year it considered the advantages of Persian, no doubt basing its consideration on the writings of Claudius Buchanan (see p. 88), who had long and close connections with the Society. After the founding of the British and Foreign Bible Society in 1809, this interest in Bible translation and literature work began to decline. But interest in Persian and Persia was kept alive by Henry Martyn's translation of the New Testament into Persian and by the story of his death in Turkey which caught the imagination of many missionary-minded people at the time and made Martyn one of the heroes of cms (so much so that keen evangelicals christened their children, Martyn, in his honour). The Society's reports of both 1815 and 1816 contain long letters from representatives of the Bible Society in Russia, outlining the advantages of providing material in Persian for the missionaries on the borders of Persia to distribute to the many merchants and others who visited such places as Astrakan, Tiflis and Shusha. In 1827, as we have seen, the Society tried to persuade Anthony Groves to go to Persia. But it was not until 1869 that a missionary of the Society was at work there and not until 1875 that the Persia Mission became formally part of the Society.

It would appear that the work in Persia began almost by accident. In 1858 Robert Bruce, a 25-year-old newly-ordained deacon from Trinity College, Dublin, was sent out to join the CMS mission at Amritsar in the Punjab. In 1862 he and Thomas Valpy French (afterwards Bishop of Lahore) were sent to start work at Derajat on the north-west frontier between India and Afghanistan. Although Pushtoo was the most common language there, Bruce found himself in contact with many Persian speakers.

In 1868 Bruce's health broke down and he was invalided home with his wife. A year later, with his health restored, he was ready to return to India, leaving his wife to follow later. Before leaving, he debated the possibility of spending some time in Persia on his way back, in order to improve his Persian. When he mentioned this to Henry Venn, the General Secretary of the Society, he was surprised to be told: 'I am so thankful for the opening, it is one of those things we looked for in vain in times past, but which God is giving us now.'

On his arrival in Isfahan, or rather its Armenian suburb of Julfa, Bruce found that one of the periodic famines was in progress and that the material and moral state of the inhabitants was quite desperate. In the summer of 1870 he was joined by his wife. The famine was at its height and before long the young couple were caring for no less than 7,000 people to whom they were giving as much relief as they could afford. Thanks to the energetic work of men like Sir Henry Rawlinson in England and Colonel Haigh in Calcutta, large sums of money were raised, which were very largely administered by the Bruces, with the assistance of the Telegraph Company's employees who were able to give relief to the many starving people they met on the roads as they travelled between the various telegraph posts. Other contributors to Bruce's relief operation were Pastor Haas, who had been for many years with the Basel mission in Tabriz (see p. 100) and was now in Stuttgart and Sir Moses Montefiore who sent £1,000 for Jewish relief. The famine conditions were not entirely due to natural causes but were in part due to the unnatural greed of the merchants who refused to sell the corn they had hoarded and to the avidity of the *mullahs*, who asked Bruce to deduct a percentage of the 6d a week which he was distributing as relief, as a religious tax. This he refused to do; but he could no nothing about the hoarding.

In the winter of 1870–1 heavy snow fell thus ensuring a good harvest for the following year, but the famine had left a large number of orphans to be cared for. Pastor Haas offered a further £1,700 for the establishment of an orphanage, but when the offer reached CMS they replied that Bruce would not be staying in Persia so the money was given to two Armenians. They tried unsuccessfully to start an orphanage in Tabriz and eventually the money, less £400, reached Bruce who started a small orphanage and industrial school in Julfa which ran for a number of years and saved the lives of many children, both Muslim and Armenian.

Meanwhile, Bruce, who had some private means and had been supporting himself in Julfa, was informed by the committee of CMS that if he was to stay in Persia he must undertake the revision of Martyn's New Testament and the translation of the rest of the Bible. To this he gladly agreed and was to devote a major portion of the rest of his time in Persia to this work. In the years that followed Bruce was frequently hard pressed for money, but his sister in Dublin collected sufficient funds for him to complete the simple building which was to serve as the mission house until 1904, when the mission moved from Julfa to Isfahan. Other friends, including some important members of the Society, supported him as individuals.

In 1871 he was asked by his Armenian neighbour to assist in the running of a small school, and this he consented to do. Naturally all the pupils were Armenian and although Bruce's aim was to work among Muslims, he found himself almost insensibly drawn into working with Armenians, thus laying himself open to the charge of proselytising from another Christian body. While the mission was so strictly confined to Julfa this seems to have been inevitable, and all that can be said is that the building up of an Armenian Protestant body was done reluctantly and abandoned as soon as conditions permitted. On the whole the Armenian authorities recognised the mission's intentions, and relations between the two bodies were for the most part friendly, although from time to time, for example in 1874, there was considerable opposition.

149

It was in 1874, however, that Bruce's first help came in the person of an Armenian, Carapet Johannes, a native of Julfa who had been educated in England at the expense of the Reverend W. Price, a CMS missionary in India. After his education and training, Johannes went to India in the employ of the Society and became headmaster of a school in Nasik. He met Bruce while he was on a visit to his relations in Julfa, and was persuaded, with the Society's permission, to stay there. It is interesting to note that even in these early days Bruce held most of his services in Persian – only the hymns and psalms being sung in Armenian.

In 1875 Bruce's work was officially recognised by the Society, and from then on he had their full backing and support. But it was not until 1880 that the first recruit came out to join him and then he was not found or paid for by CMS but by a certain Mr Edmonds of Edinburgh. He was Dr E. F. Hoernle, one of the five missionary children of the Basel missionary society's missionary, C. E. Hoernle, who on his expulsion from Russia had gone with Pfander and others to work for the CMS in India.

Young Hoernle, who had been born in India, spoke Hindustani and a little Persian when he arrived. He soon picked up the language and within eight months of his arrival we hear of him preaching in Persian. His medical work was severely limited by lack of money, so he taught in the school and as funds became available erected the simple buildings which were to form the core of the mission hospital until it moved to its present buildings in Isfahan.

The following year, 1881, Bruce and his family went home on a well-earned furlough and engaged in a strenuous campaign of recruiting and fund-raising. This deputation work did much to bring the new mission field to the attention of many more supporters, particularly in Ireland. As a result a number of earliest recruits were Irish. Bruce returned to Persia in 1882 and in 1883 he was glad to welcome his old friend and co-worker T. V. French, now Bishop of Lahore. On 18 May French confirmed sixty-seven people (all, it is believed, were Armenians), and on 20 May he ordained the Reverend Minas George deacon, the first Anglican ordination ever to be performed in Persia.

The first female missionary to join Bruce was Irish, but she was not sent out by CMS since they were not sending single female missionaries abroad at this time. She was Miss Isabella Read and she was supported by the Society for Promoting Female Education in the East. In 1852 the Society (which was founded in 1834) had been approached with a request to send out suitable teachers to teach the ladies of Isfahan and Tehran the manners and learning of the West, but had been unable to comply with the request at that time. Miss Read proved a notable addition to the mission which she served for many years both before and after her marriage to Joseph Aidiniantz, the headmaster of the school for Persian boys. She is also remembered today as the mother of two of the most famous missionaries of a later era, Miss Nouhie and Miss Nevarth Aidin.

While in Isfahan Bishop French visited the Prince Governor Zillu's-Sultan, son of Nasr-ud-din Shah and a prominent figure in the life of the mission for many years, playing a role not dissimilar to that of Shah Abbas and the Roman Catholic missionaries in the seventeenth century. The bishop was disappointed by the visit and was disconcerted by the governor's reluctance to take his earnest exhortations seriously. Nevertheless Zillu's-Sultan was well disposed towards the British. He engaged a series of tutors for his children; two of these, Mr Swift and Mr Sparrow, provided the missionaries with a little innocent amusement. Sparrow, under the name of Sparroy, wrote an account of his time as tutor, under the title *Persian Children of the Royal Family*. On occasion the mission was called on to supply temporary teaching help in the absence of Swift or Sparrow. There is no doubt that although at times – for diplomatic reasons of his own – Zillu's-Sultan had to act against the interests of the mission, on the whole his continued goodwill and that of his family has been an important factor in the establishment of the Anglican Church in Isfahan and in its acceptance as an institution in the town.

One of Bruce's actions while he was in England was to urge the establishment of an out-station of the Persia Mission in Baghdad. The mission was opened in 1883 and continued under the control of Isfahan until 1899. It seems to have contributed little to the extension of missionary work in Persia and merely resulted in additional travelling and administrative work for Bruce.

At the end of 1885 Hoernle, who during the year had lost his wife (Bruce's daughter) in childbirth, seems to have been rather pessimistic about the prospects of the mission, which he could only describe as 'fagged yet persevering'. But the work had begun and gradually the number of missionaries increased. The next time

Bruce went home he came back with a new recruit, the Reverend Henry Carless. On their way back they encountered a terrible storm on the Caspian Sea and the journey from Baku to the port of Enzeli lasted for two weeks, for the last two days of which the passengers had no food.

Single women missionaries were now being recruited by CMS and in 1889 the first two came, Miss Valpy for Baghdad, where she died within a few months of her arrival, and Miss Wilson, who joined the mission in Julfa. Also bound for Baghdad in the same sending was the Reverend C. H. Stileman, who was later transferred to Julfa. Other events of this year were the retirement of Hoernle and the visit of the intrepid Victorian traveller, Mrs Isabella Bishop, whose descriptions of the mission are of great interest. There had, it seems, been talk in England of extravagant living by missionaries and as a counterblast to this Mrs Bishop described the mission as follows:

The mission house here (Julfa) is a native building, its walls and ceilings simply decorated with pale brown arabesques on a white ground. There are a bedroom and parlour with an anteroom giving access to both from the courtyard, a store room and a kitchen. Across the courtyard are servants' quarters and a guest room for natives. Above these, reached by an outside stair, are a good room occupied by Mr Carless as a study and bedroom, and one small guest room. Another stair leads to two rooms above some of the girls' school premises, having two enclosed alcoves used as sleeping and dressing rooms. These are occupied by two ladies. One room serves as eating room for the whole mission party, at present six in number, and as a drawing room and work room. Books, a harmonium, Persian rugs on the floor and just enough furniture for use constitute its 'luxury' . . . the life all round is a very busy one. Visitors are never refused at any hour. The long flat mud roofs from which one can see the gardens and the hills are used for exercise, otherwise some of the party would never have anything better than mud walls for their horizon and life in courtyards is rather depressing for Europeans.

After pointing out that Dr Bruce and some of the other missionaries had enough private means to provide themselves with much more comfortable surroundings had they wished, Mrs Bishop goes on to discuss the difficulties of missionaries, particularly female missionaries:

Women coming to the East as missionaries are by far the greatest sufferers, especially if they are young . . . a woman cannot take a walk or a ride or go to a house without a trusty man-servant in attendance on her, and this is often inconvenient. So she does not go out at all, contenting herself with a walk on the roof or in a courtyard. The wave of enthusiasm on which a lady leaves her own country soon spends its force. . . . The enthusiastic addresses, and farewell meetings, the journey 'up-country' with its excitement and novelties and the cordial welcome from the mission circle to which she is introduced soon become things of the past. The circle, however kind, has its own interests and work and having provided her with a *munshi* (language teacher) . . . she is left to face the difficulties of languages with which ours have no affinity, in a loneliness which is all the more severely felt because she is usually for a time at least one of a family circle. Unless she is a doctor or nurse, she can do nothing till she has learnt the language . . . then she finds that the work, instead of seeking her, has to be made by her, most laboriously and oftentimes the glowing hope of telling of the Redeemer's life and death to throngs of eager and receptive listeners is fulfilled in the drudgery of teaching sewing and the rudiments of English. . . .

She then considers the plight of the missionary group as a whole:

The small group is frequently destitute of social resources outside itself, it is cut off from friendly visits, services, lectures, music, new books, news and many other recreative influences which all men regard as innocent. The life work seems at times thrown away. . . . Is it wonderful that supposed slights, tiffs, criticisms, which would be utterly brushed away if a good walk in the open or a good gallop were possible . . . should be brooded over till they attain a magnitude which embitters and depresses life?

This objective account by an acute but not unsympathetic observer seemed worth quoting at some length, since it paints the inescapable background to missionary work in Persia and elsewhere

153

at that time, and will find many an echo in the hearts of missionaries serving today. The Persia Mission has not escaped the frictions and differences she mentions. When men and women of strong personalities are compelled to live together in close proximity with little chance of escape then serious differences and difficulties are bound to occur. Many a missionary has echoed the words of a veteran American missionary in Turkey, quoted by Mrs Bishop, 'Believe me the greatest trial of missionaries is missionaries!'

A word here about the type of men and women who were recruited as missionaries by the CMS at this time may not be inappropriate. About the middle of the 1850s a second evangelical revival began, culminating in the great revival of 1859 in Northern Ireland. The young men and women who were influenced by these movements were the children of prosperous middle-class parents, who would naturally send their sons to Oxford or Cambridge and would be prepared for their daughters to accept a call to the mission field. The fact that Bruce was Irish and that the Irish Church was a minority Church face to face with a Roman Catholic majority, contributed to the peculiarly low-Church nature of the Persia Mission in its earliest days. There is no doubt that such a doctrinal position is held in a rigid and dogmatic way by people who are not likely to admit easily that they may be wrong about anything. There is no doubt also that the early missionaries were influenced by the 'holiness' teaching of the Keswick Convention and similar evangelical agencies.

So those who volunteered for service overseas were unbending rather than flexible, very certain of their own position and calling. Two other factors added to the difficulties of the situation. Firstly, the loneliness of each station and its almost complete isolation meant that when a difference of opinion arose, outside mediation was very difficult. Secondly, we need to remember that the lay missionary and his institution, either hospital or school, came before the clerical missionary and the Church, and that for a long while the Church was overshadowed by the institution. Given these facts, it is not difficult to see how friction arose and often continued for a long time, to the great disturbance of the progress of the Gospel and the building up of a Church. As one missionary was to say of Kerman, many years later, 'the wonder is not that there are so few Christians, but that there are any at all'.

The world of the early missionary was a very masculine one,

and the position of an unmarried female missionary must have been hard indeed. The education of teachers and nurses was limited to their own speciality and was not in any sense liberal. Those who came out as evangelists were often even less well educated and their piety was extremely narrow. We read of one missionary of this period whose upbringing had been so limited that she would not even countenance the reading of *Pilgrim's Progress* since this was a work of fiction. On the whole, they ministered faithfully and simply to the 'natives', but were, to a very considerable extent, incapable of really understanding them.

One further point needs to be made: the social and educational background of the missionaries and the whole ethos of the colonial epoch cut them off almost entirely from the possibility of meeting even the most educated Persians on anything like equal terms. One has only to read Sparrow's account of his time as tutor to Zillu's-Sultan's children to realise how superior every Englishman felt himself to be to even the best of the Persians and how hard it was to overcome this prejudice. It was said, many years later, that some of the early missionaries looked on the Persians much as a kind-hearted lord of the manor would look on his poorer tenants. This attitude had an important bearing on the future of the work in that it created a gulf between the missionaries and the Persians and reinforced the missionaries' opinion that a very long period would have to elapse before there was any possibility of the emergence of an indigenous leadership. It also meant that they were by instinct paternalistic and the dispensers of benevolence, rather than partners or co-workers.

One of the missionaries who triumphantly overcame all the difficulties of race and background and succeeded in identifying herself completely with the Persian women among whom she worked was Mary Bird. Grand-daughter of a distinguished Indian administrator and related to the families of Archbishop Sumner and William Wilberforce, she came to Persia in May 1891. She was not trained for anything in particular, but she had a burning desire to serve and a slight knowledge of elementary medicine (she used often to refer to herself as 'a quack'). These qualifications were sufficient in those far-off days for her to undertake to run dispensaries, which she did in spite of tremendous opposition at every level. She had one great asset besides her love for the Persians and that was good linguistic ability. She soon learnt to talk to the poorest women in their own kind of Persian and so to understand them and their needs and aspirations. The *mullahs* used every device they could think of to stop her work; they told girls who attended her class that, if they continued, they would be childless, and many believed them. On another occasion they spread the rumour that she was a Bahai. They preached against her in the mosques, they threatened the man who rented her premises, they sent roughs to try and close the dispensaries and fanatical youths threw mud and stones at her in the street. But it was of no avail; she outfaced them all and with firm courtesy refused to yield to them. She accommodated herself so completely to the Persian way of life that towards the end of her life when a new missionary was going to join her she was warned: 'You are going to have a fellow-worker who does the work of six men and lives on biscuits and eggs. Don't copy her!' There was really not much danger, such people are inimitable!

Two remarkable men joined the mission in 1894: one, newly qualified as a doctor and at the beginning of his missionary career, Dr Donald Carr (of whom more will be said later), and the other already more than middle-aged with forty-four years of missionary service behind him, Bishop Edward Craig Stuart. Stuart had gone out to Agra with T. V. French in 1850 and helped to found St John's College there. After twenty-seven years in India he was consecrated second Bishop of Waiapu in New Zealand, remaining there until, inspired by his friend French going to Muscat, the urge to serve once again as a simple missionary became too strong for him and he volunteered to come to Persia.

The twenty years between the arrival of Dr Carr and Bishop Stuart and the beginning of the First World War represent one of the key periods in the life of the mission and in the evolution of the Persian Church. It was also a key period in Persian history. The beginning of the revolutionary era which was to end in the granting of a Constitution and the establishment of a bicameral legislature with a lower house or parliament, the *Majlis*, and an upper house or Senate, may be said to have begun with the assassination of Nasr-ud-din Shah in 1896. In that same year there was a nasty riot in Isfahan over the death of two nightwatchmen in a European-owned opium factory in Julfa. It was rumoured that either the Armenians or the Europeans had murdered them. A mob stormed the gates of Julfa and for nearly a week there were disturbances in the town. But this was only an isolated incident; the new Shah, Muzaffaradin Shah, came to the throne and things seemed to go on much as usual.

In 1897 Carless went to Kerman on a trial basis. After eight months there, he recommended that it should be occupied as a mission station on a permanent basis. So in April 1898 Mr and Mrs A. R. Blackett, who were Australians from Melbourne, took up permanent residence there. In May 1898 Carless caught typhoid and Dr Carr had to make an epic six-day ride to reach him. He reported that Carless was for the most part wandering or in a coma, but shortly before he died he had a lucid spell, and a bright smile, as though he were recognising a friend, crossed his face. Carr was convinced that Carless had seen a vision of Jesus and used frequently to relate this event.

Another outstanding missionary of the epoch was the Reverend Napier Malcolm of New College, Oxford, who joined the mission in 1898. He was appointed to Yezd to work as pastor of the church alongside Dr Henry White who had been there since the previous April. In 1899 they were joined by Miss Mary Bird, Dr Urania Latham and Miss Brighty. The governor of Yezd was the eldest son of Zillu's-Sultan and thus well disposed towards the missionaries. A few years later Sir Percy Sykes, the British Consul in Yezd, reported the changes which the missionaries' presence had brought about there. In a lecture to the Royal Geographical Society he said: 'Thanks to the unwearying devotion of Dr White of the CMS and his staff and to the fair-dealing of our countrymen, the townspeople have been changed from fanatical opponents of Europeans into adopting a friendly attitude, the recently-constructed hospital being daily thronged.' Malcolm set about starting a school for boys and observing the Yezdis with that penetrating understanding which later enabled him to write his book, *Five Years in a Persian Town*, which provides an unrivalled insight into what it felt like to live in this remote desert town at the beginning of the twentieth century.

Prior to his return to England on sick-leave in 1898, Dr Carr had become famous in Isfahan as a skilful and trustworthy doctor. He was patronised by many of the wealthy people of the town and by the Prince Governor and his family. He was also much in demand amongst the Bakhtiari tribespeople. Both he and subsequent mission doctors paid them frequent visits and there seems little doubt that the pronounced pro-British tendencies for which the

157

Bakhtiaris were famous were at least in part due to the readiness of the missionary doctors to care for their leaders whenever they were needed.

Dr Julian Bharier in his recent book, *Economic Development in Iran 1900–1970*, has given us a clear picture of the general state of Iran in 1900. The population was just under 10,000,000 and the average expectation of life was under thirty years. Ninety per cent of the population was engaged in agriculture and there was nothing that could be properly called a factory. Apart from a mere 800 miles of road (mainly in the north), all roads were mule tracks and entirely unsuitable for wheeled traffic. The author concludes: 'There were signs that the economy was developing but at the turn of the century it still remained one of the most backward countries in the world.'

In 1901 Dr Carr made an interesting comparison of the hospital as it was when he came out to take it over in 1894 and as it was in 1901. When he came he found the hospital in a very bad state of repair, more like a caravanserai than a hospital, with only three wards accommodating six men and seven women. In 1901 there was an entire wing for women and beds for twenty-three men. In 1894 there was no nursing staff, each patient being looked after by a friend or relative. In 1901 nursing care had been revolutionised by the Canadian sister, Helen McKim. In 1894 there was a minimum of hygiene and cleanliness and the patients remained in their own clothes, which were often torn and filthy. In 1901 they had clean linen and clean hospital garments and there was a high standard of antisepsis in the hospital. Between 500 and 600 patients passed through the hospital during the year 1900, with an average stay of fourteen days.

Throughout this period the missionaries came up against the followers of the Bab, known to them as Babis and to us as Bahais, a heretical Muslim sect which had been founded in 1852 and had grown and multiplied amongst the depressed lower-middle-class Jews, Zoroastrians and Muslims. From their earliest days they had been relentlessly and harshly persecuted and outbreaks against them were always liable to occur. One such persecution broke out in Yezd in 1903. It started with the killing of a single man in June, and broke out again a few days later with a mass attack against all who were suspected of holding such a heresy. It is symptomatic of the disturbed state of the times and the weakness of those in authority that the governor and the police were powerless to stop the rioting. Dr White was called to the house of a wounded Babi. While he was treating him the mob broke into the house and killed two more men. Dr White's patient died of shock but Dr White was unhurt – the crowd shouting that they had no quarrel with foreigners. The missionaries did what they could to shelter the Babis and Malcolm, whose day-to-day account of the massacres still survives, seems to have shown considerable courage in protecting those in danger.

Owing to the extreme isolation of Yezd the rioting did not spread to any other towns. It was in this year that this isolation was slightly lessened by the opening of the Central Persian branch of the telegraph line of the Indo-European Telegraph Company, which linked together Kerman, Yezd and Isfahan. The line and the service were erratic; the tribespeople used to use the insulators for firing practice and it was not unknown for missionaries to send a telegram announcing their impending departure for Isfahan and being asked to take the telegram with them when they set out a few days later. But it did mark the beginning of the end of the complete isolation which separated the various mission stations.

During this period the Reverend St Clair Tisdall established his reputation as a first-class linguist and scholar. In 1894 he bought a small printing press, which he named the Henry Martyn Memorial Press, and with it he produced a considerable number of books, simple textbooks for the schools, portions of the Bible in various dialects, as well as a number of tracts. He thought it advisable, however, to have the more controversial tracts printed in India. He pursued his study of languages, learning classical Armenian as well as the Julfa dialect, and composed his Persian conversation grammar which is still in print today. In 1902 he was awarded an honorary doctorate by Edinburgh University, 'in recognition of his contributions to philological science'.

Late in 1903 Dr Carr's many contacts with the sick in Isfahan whom he used to visit after dark bore fruit. He was offered the chance of purchasing cheaply about six acres of land on which the wealthy owner said he could build a hospital. This was the successful conclusion of a prolonged effort to establish the mission in Isfahan itself. Bishop Stuart had had a house there since 1893 and had lived there from time to time. At one time it was closed for a short period on the orders of the governor, but was soon reopened through the intervention of Preece, the Consul, and the British Minister in Tehran and from then on it was more or less permanently occupied. Funds for the purchase of the land for the hospital, then outside the town but now in the fashionable street of Abbas Abad, were raised mainly in England and in New Zealand (from where a friend of Bishop Stuart, Archdeacon Williams, sent £1,100).

In February 1904 the out-patients' department of the new hospital was completed. Up to that time some rooms in Bishop Stuart's house had been used for this purpose. The vacant rooms were soon occupied by the school for Persian boys, which had eight pupils when it moved from Julfa. Its numbers very soon trebled and early in 1905 Mr Allison, the first lay missionary sent out by CMS and superintendent of the school, also took up residence in Isfahan. The men's side of the hospital was completed in October 1904 and the move from Julfa took place. The women followed in April 1906, when their department was completed.

The bicycle was a very popular mode of transport among the missionaries. Dr Carr made an epic bicycle journey one year from Enzeli to Isfahan. We also read of Mr and Mrs Stileman completing a tour of 862 miles to Yezd and Kerman on their bicycles in the summer of 1904, and Mr Stileman then going the 425 miles back to Kerman once more to relieve the pressure of work there – and all this on mere tracks across the desert, since there was nothing that could be called a road, with or without a metalled surface. The use of bicycles continued well on into the 1930s and older missionaries still remember with regret the days when they could freely go about their business on bicycles in Isfahan and Yezd – something which would not be so easy today.

The fortunes of the mission in the years 1906–19 were largely dependent on the larger events of history which were entirely beyond the missionaries' control. The period was marked by great political upheavals, general increase in lawlessness and frequent breakdown of all local authority. The attitude towards foreigners fluctuated; sometimes, as Napier Malcolm pointed out: 'Governors are glad of the presence in the towns of any element that can be used as a set-off to the fanaticism of the *mullahs*. A medical mission or even under some circumstances a successful school may therefore receive the support of a governor who is himself a thorough Muhammedan.'

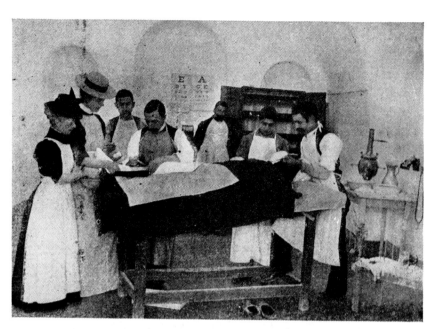

6a. Dr Henry White operating in the Yezd hospital.

b. Miss Isabella Read and Armenian girls from her school in Julfa, c. 1890.

7a. *Top*:   Zillu's-Sultan and his favourite son, Akbar Mirza (Sareme Dowleh).
 b. *Bottom*: Bishop Stuart and members of the C.M.S. mission in Isfahan.
     c. 1904 (see p. 163).

Meanwhile the opposition of the religious leaders continued, and in 1907 during *Muharram*, the month of mourning, the *mullahs* conducted a violent campaign of preaching against the missionaries and all their works. The annual report for this year concluded: 'The condition of Persia throughout the year was lamentable.' In a letter reviewing the situation at this time, Dr Carr gives a vivid picture of what the constitutional movement meant to the people of Isfahan.

'When the year opened,' he wrote, 'the parliament (in Tehran) was in full swing. A state of things came about which could not be satisfactory and could not last. Every town had its own assembly and wished to be as far as possible independent. It was a case of Home Rule all round. In Isfahan there was not only one central assembly but there were a dozen or more small local self-constituted assemblies at which a great deal of talking was done, though not much else. The main idea of the people with regard to a Constitution seemed to be that it was a form of government under which no one need pay any taxes and everyone might do as he liked.'

Small wonder that highway robbery and violence of every kind were on the increase and that all the mission hospitals reported an increasing number of gunshot wounds among their patients. In 1909 the Bakhtiari chiefs gained control of Isfahan and marched on Tehran. The Shah took refuge in the Russian Embassy and was deposed, his place being taken by his 13-year-old son.

Meanwhile the mission grew in numbers and seeming influence, and the powers of religious reaction and fanaticism seemed to be on the wane. A new missionary, J. H. Linton, reported from Shiraz that when the governor executed some rebels during the month of Ramazan a prominent *mullah* in the town protested. The governor reacted by sending him some photographs of the execution of Sheikh Fazlullah in Tehran with a curt note to the effect that Sheikh Fazlullah was a great deal more important than he was. No more was heard of the complaint.

In 1909 Bishop Stuart resigned after fifteen years in Persia and fifty-nine years in all on the mission field. He was an extraordinarily able man and impressed everyone by his exceptional tolerance and broadmindedness which did not conflict in the least with his determination to bring the Gospel to those who had never heard it. He died two years later in England. Bishop Stuart never had full episcopal powers in Persia, which was still under the titular jurisdiction of the Bishop of London. But in 1913 a great step forward was taken in the life of the Church in Persia when it was constituted a fully independent diocese of the Anglican Church and the Reverend C. H. Stileman was consecrated its first bishop. It must be admitted, however, that this was more an act of faith than a response to a felt need. The general condition of the country was still bad and during the past few years there had been widespread unrest and anti-foreign feeling which resulted in the lapsing of a number of converts. The organised Church scarcely existed as such and the few Persian Christians who remained faithful were very much overshadowed by the missionaries and the missionary institutions. The period of indigenisation had not yet begun and it is sad that just as a missionary could write in his annual letter for 1913 : 'For the first time for several years it is possible to report some improvement in the condition of Persia', another upheaval was at hand which was to retard the growth of the Persian Church by at least twenty years. The outbreak of war in August 1914 did not immediately seem to have much effect on the work of the mission. W. J. Thompson arrived to take up work in the Persian boys' school which had moved to new premises in the shadow of the Shah Mosque and a hostel had been opened with six boys. The government gave the hospital in Isfahan a grant of £50 which just about covered the amount it had paid in customs duty on imported medicines. All seemed to be going well.

But in 1915, the year in which Robert Bruce and Mary Bird died, German influence began to make itself felt and attacks instigated by the German spy, Wassmuss, were made on British officials in Bushire, Shiraz and Isfahan. In September 1915 the British were ordered to evacuate south Persia and the missionaries were scattered, some going to India, some only as far as Ahwaz, and some to England. Others took up various kinds of war work in different parts of the Middle East. Both Yezd and Kerman hospitals were visited by German soldiers in 1915 and closed temporarily, but were opened again in 1916. By the middle of 1916, eight of the missionaries had returned to Isfahan, which had been occupied by the Russians in May of that year. By August 1916 the situation in the south had so much improved that Dr Carr and Mr Linton were able to pay a fifteen-day visit to Soulat-ud-Dowleh,

the leader of the Qashqai tribe, who, the missionaries were surprised to find, received Reuter's telegrams regularly and sub-
scribed to the daily edition of *The Times*.

The immediate post-war period was marked by famine conditions followed by typhus, cholera and influenza and by a great increase in malarial infections, all of which took a terrible toll of the
population and many families who had previously been moderately
well-off were reduced to complete beggary. Under such circumstances it is not surprising that a missionary could sum up the position of the tiny Church at this time in the following way: 'The
Church has not yet learnt to walk alone and many of the converts
while appreciating the benefits of Christianity, fail to practise its
precepts in daily life.'

Another feature that weakened the life of the Church was the
infiltration of a number of Bahais who, while quite willing to con-
fess belief in all the tenets of Christianity, secretly retained their
Bahai faith and propagated it among the members of the little
Church. It seems certain that the missionaries were not always alert
to this danger and tended to accept all the professions of faith which
were made to them.

Bishop Stileman had been ill for some time and in 1915 had been
forced to resign because of ill health. He was not replaced until
1919 when his place was taken by Bishop J. H. Linton.

Plate 7(*b*). Names from left to right: *Standing*: Mr Johannes, Miss Buncher,
Rev. C. H. Stileman, Miss Ward, Mr Allinson and child, Dr E. Stuart, Dr
Ironside, Dr Carr, Miss Petley.
Sitting: Mrs Allinson, Miss McKim, Mrs Stileman, Bishop Stuart, Miss A.
Stuart, Miss Braine-Hartnell, Mrs Carr, Nora Carr, Mr Biddlecombe.
On ground: Miss Proctor, Miss M. Stuart, Rev. Walker and child, Margaret
Carr.

Chapter Fourteen

THE C.M.S. IN PERSIA
PART II: 1919-1961

The years between the end of the war and 1926 saw the final collapse of the Qajar dynasty and the rise to power of Reza Khan, who was chosen by an overwhelming majority of the people as the new Shah and hence the founder of the new Pahlavi dynasty.

This change was of fundamental importance for the future of the country. Once more Persia was able to produce a man of heroic gifts, who could lift his country out of apathy and backwardness and inspire her people to make the necessary efforts to modernise their country, to utilise their vast natural resources, and to mobilise their great – though latent – abilities. The war had lowered the prestige of all the European nations in Persian eyes and the time was ripe for an appeal to national pride, and this was what Reza Shah made. Most of his efforts were directed to encouraging his countrymen to stand on their own feet and to make the most of what they had, instead of letting it be exploited by foreigners.

In 1919 the mission was surprisingly well staffed. Besides Bishop Linton who had been consecrated that year and his wife (formerly Dr Alicia Aldous), there were three married clergy and two single ordained men, four married doctors and five single doctors, of whom three were women, and seventeen unmarried women, the majority of whom were teachers or nurses. Such an abundance of staff, particularly of doctors, was never to occur again. As they retired, the Society was not able to replace them and a shortage of doctors became a permanent feature of the missionary situation.

In spite of the political uncertainty which overshadowed the mission (as noted by Linton in 1920), the missionaries (especially the doctors) were full of hope. Village itineration was still possible; frequent trips were made by the doctors and the evangelists to the villages surrounding Isfahan, Yezd and Kerman. But the view expressed by Dr Carr in 1920 was becoming more and more widely held: 'We realise that Europeans can do little for the evangelisation of Persia. More and more their work is to train others.'

No one understood the new spirit in the country and the new responsibilities it would bring to the Church better than Bishop Linton. His experience as a young missionary in Africa and his later experience in Iran had convinced him that the raising up of a national ministry was the prime task that lay before him as bishop. He went about it with a speed and energy that was not universally acceptable. Some of the older missionaries felt that his actions were too precipitate and his choices ill-judged. Was it really right to ordain a man who had formerly been 'a mere cigarette-seller'? Perhaps not, but surely the principle was right and it was certainly in conformity with the aspirations of the Persians as a whole. Setbacks and failures occurred in the Church, as they did in other walks of life, but the first steps so taken – though faltering – were certainly in the right direction.

In 1921 a much loved missionary, Dr Catherine Ironside, who had caught a chill while visiting the Jewish quarter in Isfahan, died of pneumonia. She was buried in the Armenian cathedral at Julfa as a gesture of respect and affection by the Armenian community among whom she had worked for many years. This gesture was a symbol of the improved relations between the two communities which had been brought about by Bishop Linton's visit to the Armenian Archbishop earlier the same year, when he promised that the missionaries would no longer accept Armenians into the Anglican Church. This assurance went far to relieve the age-long suspicion of the Armenians when confronted with foreign missionaries.

Linton's moves towards a slightly less rigid Protestantism resulted in a certain amount of friction between him and some of the older missionaries. His wish to have a cross on the communion table, when hitherto there had never been one, was not universally acceptable. So perhaps it was providential that in 1922 the Telegraph Company's doctor in Shiraz retired and the Company asked the mission if they would take over the supervision of the health of their employees. The terms they offered were generous and made it possible for Shiraz to be restarted as a mission station and for some of the older missionaries, who had not seen eye to eye with the bishop, to go down there to open up medical work. The party finally consisted of Dr and Mrs Carr and their daughter Margaret (later Mrs. W. J. Thompson), Dr Emmeline Stuart, Miss Braine Hartnell, Miss Thomas and Sister Alice Verinder, all of whom (with the exception of Miss Carr and Sister Alice Verinder) had been missionaries in Persia for over twenty years.

The early days of the work in Shiraz were difficult; quarters were cramped, drugs were in short supply, but the people crowded in and some times 250 were seen in a morning. Eventually a house was found and converted, and Dr Carr and Dr Stuart, who were already well known in the town, settled down to consolidate the medical work.

The hopes of the missionaries were confirmed by a number of events in 1922 and 1923. The bishop had bought a car, and so the time needed for travelling round the diocese was reduced enormously. At Whitsun in 1923 Dr Schaffter (a member of the famous missionary family from India) together with two Persian men and two Persian women were licensed as lay readers. Schaffter afterwards served the hospital in Isfahan for many years, and became famous for his theological knowledge and his sermons. During the same visit of the bishop to Kerman no less than fifteen adults and eight infants were baptised.

In October 1923 the first Diocesan conference was held in Isfahan; its main activities were the discussion of the possibilities of union with the Presbyterian Church and the drafting of a constitution for the Church. This provisional constitution reduced the powers of the mission and gave greater responsibility to the Church through the various committees and boards which were set up. The prospects of union, which in those early days seemed very bright, were to fade as the years went by. The reasons are complex but they include the predominance in the northern Church of Assyrians and Armenians who worship in their own languages, and the imbalance between the financial strength of the two Churches, which made the northern Church feel that it would be giving up much and receiving far less in return. The question of the episcopal form of government was naturally a cause for concern, but it never seems to have been a dominant issue, or at least not amongst the Persian members of the Presbyterian Church.

Hospitals and schools were still flourishing, though the hospitals were soon to be affected by the shortage of staff and the inability of the Society in London to find and finance suitable replacements as the various doctors retired or resigned. In 1922 the Isfahan schools had 120 boys and 50 girls. In Yezd under Miss Aidin and in Kerman under Miss Janet Woodroffe schools flourished and performed a most useful function, giving their pupils a first taste of freedom and limited independence. In 1924 a new recruit arrived, in the person of the Reverend R. N. Sharp, who was to play a prominent part in the life of the Church for nearly forty years. Sharp was a scholar and an artist. He rapidly acquired an excellent knowledge of the language and a love for the country, its art, architecture and literature, all of which he studied closely. Like many other missionaries before him, Sharp was a great builder. The church in Yezd where he began his ministry was his work, but was unfortunately destroyed by flood in 1941. But the church in Shiraz which was finally opened in 1938 is his masterpiece and still stands as an example of a building which is truly Christian in design but also truly Persian, down to the last detail of its fittings and ornaments. Sharp was an amateur musician of some ability and composed a number of hymn tunes in the Persian mode for the church. He also learned the old Persian language of Pahlavi and taught it at the University of Shiraz.

1926, the year of the General Strike in England, was a year of financial stringency for all the missionary societies and the Persian Mission's hopes of early reinforcements were dashed by the Society's request for retrenchment in all departments. But 1926 also saw the coronation of Reza Shah and the beginning, in real earnest, of a new age for Iran. The mission shared in the optimism which gradually became widespread in the country and from now on the name of Reza Shah appears often in the missionaries' letters. They too tried to push the country forward in some small ways. Besides the concern which they had shown for the carpet weavers of Kerman, which resulted in a code of employment for children being agreed upon by the carpet dealers, the missionaries also sent a petition to the Shah asking him to raise the age at which girls could get married, thus mitigating the harm done to health and morals by child marriages. It seems likely that such requests on the part of foreigners who were also missionaries was unlikely to be listened to by a new and nationalistic government, and nothing was changed until many years later. This action on the part of the missionaries is indicative of the way in which they still viewed their role at this time.

The new government was not slow in trying to get a grip on

the country and to bring all the various semi-independent and widely-differing forms of schools, hospitals, medical practitioners, etc., under some unified form of central control. Prior to this time the mission schools, in default of a nationally accepted diploma, had issued their own; for example in Kerman Miss Woodroffe issued a 'CMS Primary Schools Persian Certificate'. In 1927 the first school crisis arose over this and the related matter of religious teaching in schools, but was settled amicably. In 1928 the government decided to regularise the practice of medical men by instituting a Board of Medical Examiners. A missionary doctor, Dr E. F. Molony, served on the Board in Isfahan. In Shiraz a missionary doctor there at the time relates the story of the Persian doctor who, when asked what his qualifications were, took the Board members out to the cemetery and pointing to the graves said 'Half of these are my responsibility and I learnt something from every one of them'. *Si non e vero e ben trovato!*

This same year, 1928, also saw the publication of the first part of the new Civil Code of Laws which included the abolition of capitulations, which had given all foreigners, including missionaries, special privileges in the country. The missionaries did not seem to resent this and the new generation of missionaries who came out after the war were strongly impressed by the new spirit which was abroad in the country and seemed for a time at least to have shared in the general euphoria.

They also began to note among hospital patients an increasing interest in literature, and in 1927 under the inspiration of the Reverend H. E. J. Biggs, who also started a Persian Christian magazine *Omid* (Hope), a Diocesan literature committee was formed. Biggs later gained distinction as a conchologist and his work on the shells of Iran is an important contribution to science. In 1929 an Inter-church literature committee was founded under the control of the Presbyterian missionary Dr William Wysham and later Dr John Elder – the latter contributed a number of important works to its programme.

The control of the government over the dissident forces in the country was by no means complete, and in 1929 the Qashqai tribesmen raided Shiraz and the town was cut off from all outside communication for some days. It is significant, however, that the only means of communication which remained was by air, so air-mail letters continued to get through.

The educational work continued to flourish, and in Isfahan a girls' school (at first known as the Stileman Memorial School – now the Behesht Ayin School) was opened. In 1930 the Stuart Memorial College, which had started using the Government Primary Certificate the previous year, was disturbed by the death of one of the volunteer members of staff, Clifford Harris, who contracted typhoid while nursing sick villagers. Harris was representative of the best type of missionary volunteer at this time – a public-school boy with great physical strength and a sincere belief in public-school values and a simple but very firmly held Christian faith, which won the affection and respect of all the Persians with whom he came in contact.

The Yezd and Kerman stations continued to flourish; the hospitals were gradually enlarged and in the 1930s the schools reached their highest peak of numbers and efficiency. Converts, however, were few and those who came forward were subjected to considerable persecution and, in the case of two young soldiers in Kerman in 1930, were actually imprisoned and forbidden to attend church.

In 1931 the government forbade the practice of village evangelism. However it was continued up to the beginning of the Second World War in spite of the ban. But this was really the end of an epoch. The missionaries were beginning to realise that life had changed but not necessarily for the benefit of their work. Thompson, now head of the Stuart Memorial College, wrote in 1931 somewhat regretfully : 'the age of the foreign advisers is past', and Miss Nouhie Aidin in the same year wrote : 'our greatest opponent to the Gospel is now not Islam, but indifference and materialism'.

In 1932 a new school crisis arose when a government edict was promulgated that prohibited Persian subjects of whatever religion from attending any primary school run by foreigners. This meant that all mission primary schools had to close, including the newly-opened preparatory classes of the Stuart Memorial College. However the College did obtain official recognition as a middle school and a compromise solution to the problem was reached. But the nationalist feeling was still very much in evidence and the girls' school in Shiraz, which had been opened by Miss Ella Gerard, met with fierce opposition – an opposition in which nationalist and religious elements were somewhat incongruously mixed.

169

However, the rise of a sense of pride in being a Persian had its beneficial results and as was pointed out by a new young missionary, the Reverend Geoffrey Rogers, 'the centre of gravity is shifting from the mission to the Persian Church'. He also wrote expressing clearly the missionaries' dilemma at this time:

The best and most vital manhood is deeply nationalistic. This sort of man will not accept the very first claims of the Church's message because it is connected with the foreigner. Indeed almost without exception the men whom we touch are of the sort who themselves carry no weight with their fellows . . . those whom we do try to push ahead on their own find their connection with us a drawback.

Throughout this period the government did much to improve communications in the country; a railway from the Caspian Sea to the oilfields was built and many roads were improved, although asphalting was not to come for many years. The Church profited by this improvement. In 1933 Rogers organised a successful six-weeks inter-church summer school in Isfahan which enabled church members from the north and the south to get to know one another better. It was the forerunner of a series of such meetings, which have continued regularly up to the present time.

The progress towards the indigenisation of the Church was slow and when in 1933 the first synod of the Church was held in Yezd all but one of those who attended were foreign. In 1935 Bishop Linton resigned and his place as Bishop was taken by the Reverend W. J. Thompson. In the same year the Reverend Jolinoos Hakim and the Reverend Adl Nakhosteen, the Bible Society's representative, were ordained.

In the few years that were left before the outbreak of the Second World War the work continued much as it had before, with reasons for hope and despair about equally balanced. On the one hand, the government seemed if anything anti-Islamic: *Muharram* processions were banned and the *mullahs* were subjected to considerable limitation of their power and influence. Jews, Christians and Zoroastrians were entitled to equal treatment with their Muslim fellow citizens – at least in theory. But the nationalistic feeling meant that foreigners were resented, and the propaganda of the various powers gave rise to a sense of unrest and suspicion. In 1936 a report gave the following impression: 'The new spirit of progress and independence which often shows itself in resenting any outside interference is beginning to make itself felt in our Church. The function of the missionary is no longer leadership but co-operation.' Inquirers were few and one senses a feeling verging on hopelessness in the letters of the missionaries at this time. The bright dawn of the new regime was being rapidly overcast by the clouds of a new world conflict. However, some progress was made. In 1936 the new revised prayer book was printed by Sharp in Yezd and a church was consecrated at the mountain village of Qalat near Shiraz. More and more the missionaries felt their role was changing. H. C. (David) Gurney, a newly-arrived missionary from Australia, wrote at this time: 'Under the present regime in Iran, we either work in institutions or leave the country.' Once more the age-old Persian method of dealing with foreign religions by enclosing them and encapsulating them within the walls of their own buildings was in evidence. In accordance with this new feeling of realism and self-examination, the Church registers were examined and the estimate of the number of Persian members for the churches in Shiraz, Isfahan, Kerman and the oilfields, whither a number of Christians had gone, was reduced from 600 to 350.

Staff shortages continued and the death of Dr Dodson in Kerman in 1937 raised in an acute form the whole problem of shortage of staff, which was being felt in the schools and hospitals. During this and the following year the Yezd hospital was temporarily closed for lack of staff. Nevertheless the work went on and the principal of the Stuart Memorial College, the Reverend Reg. Iliff, could write in 1939: 'The year has seen the SMC on a peak of success.'

The outbreak of yet another World War was soon to 'finish' all hopes of continuing progress. Suspicion increased, and the pro-German sympathies of many and the apparent failure of the Allies in the prosecution of the war made the life of the missionaries very hard. In addition, rising prices made living very expensive and even bread was scarce at times.

Polish refugees arrived in the country and were accommodated in the hospitals. The German Christoffel school for the blind was taken over by the Church. A few new missionaries continued to arrive. In 1941 Dr and Mrs E. B. (Peter) Wild arrived after a dangerous six-months sea journey to take up work in Kerman. But the position was obviously one of holding on until the end of the war, and soon all travel outside the country became virtually impossible. As if the war was not sufficiently disruptive, a flash flood hit Yezd in 1941 and the church and hospital were destroyed and work there had to be abandoned. In 1943 there was an epidemic of typhus in which Sister Nightingale of the Isfahan hospital died. Many of the missionaries, including Dr Stella Henriques in Shiraz and the Reverend Arthur Howden in Kerman, were engaged in relief work.

One of the happier results of the war was the adoption by the diocese, under the Orphaned Missions scheme, of the Christoffel Blindenmission. This mission had been founded many years previously by a German confessional Pastor Christoffel. At the outbreak of war he established a house in Tabriz under a German worker, Fräulein Hanni Harms, and another in Isfahan where he himself was in charge. Fräulein Harms was arrested by the Russians when they took Tabriz and interned, and the blind children were sent to Isfahan, where eventually Pastor Christoffel was also interned. The diocese were asked to carry on the work. This they did until 1945 when Bishop Thompson felt the urgent need for a trained worker. Having obtained a grant for three years from the Royal National Institute for the Blind, he was fortunate enough to recruit the services of Miss Gwen Gaster, who had been a county organiser for the blind in England.

Pastor Christoffel was eventually released and returned to Iran where he served for another five years up to his death. The work was divided: the German Society taking on the care of the boys and men and the diocese being responsible for the women and children. The institution was known as the *Nur Ayin* or House of Light. As the years passed relations between the two bodies grew closer, until now (1972) the German-sponsored work has come completely under the control of the diocese. Miss Gaster built up the work and set a new standard of blind care in Iran. Three girls have attended the University of Tehran and others are employed as telephonists, teachers, masseuses, etc. Boys have also met with the same success. Moreover, an eye clinic has been opened in Isfahan, staffed by German volunteer nurses and an Iranian specialist trained in Germany. Since Miss Gaster's retirement in 1964 the work has been ably carried on by her former deputy, Miss Dorothy Shillaker, who, with the help of Miss Ruth Mohan and a number of volunteers from Europe, Jordan and Africa, has maintained and extended the work.

The end of the war found the Church small and very under-staffed both by missionaries and by national clergy, of whom there were only four at this time – all elderly and one retired.

Lawlessness great increased and in 1946 we read of Sharp being robbed in the vestry of Qalat church by armed tribesmen. In 1950 the report from Kerman simply stated: 'it is a miracle that there are any Christians at all'. Other Churches no doubt felt much the same. Slowly the work began again and missionaries who had not been away for seven or eight years went on leave and returned refreshed; but very few new missionaries were to come for several years.

In 1951 the threat of the closing of the oilfields hung over Persia and once more the Church was faced with a crisis, not of its own making but one which nevertheless was to cause serious disruption and difficulties in its work for the next three years. The history of this episode has been amply documented elsewhere. Here, it is sufficient to say that most of the missionaries were denied access to the country for a number of years and that Bishop Thompson was expelled. Sharp was likewise ordered to leave the country but by delaying tactics he managed to remain until in 1954 the situation changed: the Shah returned and stability was restored. The hospitals similarly managed narrowly to escape closure, and the missionaries were greatly encouraged as they saw clearly the hand of God in the failure of their enemies to bring about the total destruction of their work – as they had undoubtedly hoped to do.

It was at this time that the remaining schools were removed from the control of the Church. As the crisis passed, the Church, both missionaries and nationals, were more and more conscious of the need for indigenous leadership and it was at this time that the present leaders of the Church came to the fore.

The most remarkable of the new leaders who rose to prominence in the post-war period was undoubtedly Hassan Dehqani-Tafti, whose story can be read in his short autobiography, *Design of My World*. This presents a moving picture of how a village boy from a poor family near Yezd could, by virtue of his own talents and a strong faith in God, rise to be head of the little Church and provide it with the truly Persian leadership which it had lacked for so long.

Following the lead of Dehqani-Tafti, a number of other young men, such as Arastoo Sayyah, Nosratullah Sharifian and a little later Iraj Muttehedeh, Khodadad Khosravi and then Khalil Razmara also responded to the call for Persian pastors. They are now active in the Church's ministry and provide solid hope for the future.

In 1952 all hospital and school work had closed in Kerman. A missionary writing at the time gave the following explanation: 'It seems to be largely the result of extreme nationalism expressing itself in disloyalty and a desire to have an Irani Church organised by themselves with no money from foreigners.' One may regret that no word was said at this time about the failure of the missionaries themselves to provide an adequate presentation of the Gospel to the Persians of Kerman, though there is no doubt that they were all acutely conscious of this failure. By 1955 the Churches in Kerman and Yezd had virtually ceased to exist as organised communities, although in both places those few who remained faithful met together and did what they could to keep Church life going.

After the closure of all Church schools it seemed as if educational work was to remain in abeyance almost indefinitely. However, in 1955 Miss Nouhie Aidin, at the request of some of the Christian parents in Isfahan, opened a small class which gradually grew until by 1958 it had four classes of the primary school cycle. It is from this small beginning that the present happy position of having complete primary and secondary boys' and girls' schools arose. In 1958 the writer of this book and his wife opened the boys' hostel in Isfahan to which over the years many old boys of the Stuart Memorial College have sent their children.

In October 1957 the Diocese decided (with the consent of the Presbyterian Church) to open a Church centre in Tehran, where there were a number of Anglican Christians both Persian and expatriate. The Reverend David Gurney was to serve there for the next thirteen years. In 1959 the retirement of Bishop Thompson became inevitable and Archbishop MacInnes from Jerusalem visited the diocese to sound out the opinions of Church leaders and missionaries about the appointment of his successor. As a result of his inquiries, it was felt abroad that another expatriate bishop should be appointed for a limited number of years. But at the Diocesan Council that year it was unanimously agreed that a Persian bishop should be appointed and that Bishop Hassan was the man to fill that position. The powers-that-be graciously yielded to the wish of the diocese and Bishop Hassan was consecrated in Jerusalem and enthroned in Isfahan in 1961.

The subsequent ten years since Bishop Hassan's consecration have abundantly confirmed the wisdom of the Church's decision. The recent celebrations of the 2,500th anniversary of the Persian monarchy at which Bishop Hassan was present and during which he was, with other world religious leaders, presented to his Imperial Majesty the Shah, would seem to indicate that the Protestant Churches have been accepted as an integral and permanent part of the religious life of Iran.

SMALLER SOCIETIES AND SUPPORTING BODIES

BCMS

The work of the Bible Churchmen's Missionary Society, which was originally a breakaway group from the CMS, started with the arrival of Mr and Mrs Henry Ward as young, self-supporting, unattached missionaries, in Sistan (now Zabol) in September 1925. With exemplary faith they set out from Quetta for Sistan, and eventually chose Duzdab (now Zahedan) as their location. On the arrival of Henry Ward's brother, William, as a missionary of the BCMS, the mission formally became part of BCMS work. In May 1926 Bishop Linton visited the area and requested BCMS to start work there. In December 1926 the group was joined by the Reverend George Malcolm, son of the Reverend Napier Malcolm of Yezd. They soon established the normal pattern of missionary work: dispensary, village itineration and Bible lessons for any who cared to accept them, as well as the distribution of tracts and Bible portions.

In 1927 the political situation was tense and new recruits were held up in Quetta, but by May 1928 Miss Jacobs, a nurse, and Miss Ginn had joined them. Hopes of opening a hospital in the area were indefinitely delayed and Dr Rice, who had come to run it, moved to Mirzapur in India. Police surveillance at the time made travel difficult, but nevertheless a limited amount of itineration was carried out. New recruits were also added, in the persons of Mr Brenchley and Miss Duckworth.

In 1929 things began to look a little brighter. An Indian Christian doctor, Dr Sitralka, had been found to replace Dr Rice. British consular officials were helpful and a programme of medical work embracing such widely separated places as Sistan, Birjand

and Bampur was envisaged. In the autumn of 1930 Reza Shah visited Duzdab and ordered that the name of the town be changed to Zahedan. Dr Ward was presented to him and hopes were raised. But the difficulties were so great that the work was only carried on for another four years. The missionaries gradually left and were relocated until eventually only Dr Sitralka was left to carry on loyally – which he did until the hospital was expropriated at the time of Mussadegh. Thereafter he and his wife carried on preventive work in Tehran amongst those suffering from eye diseases. With American help a clinic was opened there, which continues to function in spite of Dr Sitralka's death.

The International Mission
An inter-denominational American-based missionary society has been at work for some years, helping in the orphanage at Faraman (see p. 140) and running a Bible correspondence course and the Tehran Bible Church.

The Lutheran Orient Mission
In 1910 members of this small American mission began work in and around Tabriz, concentrating particularly on the Kurds. By 1935 their numbers had been reduced to three, and on the outbreak of war their work was abandoned. They have, however, renewed their contacts with Iran and are now helping to support Dr Richard Gardiner and the Christian hospital at Qorveh, in Persian Kurdistan. This work is also supported by the WEC (the World Evangelistic Crusade).

Numerous other bodies are at work in Iran mainly concentrating on the English-speaking or already Christian part of the population.

THE BIBLE IN PERSIAN

The earliest version of the Bible known to Persia was the *Diatessaron* or Harmony of the Gospels made by Tatian (see p. 17). This was, of course, written in Syriac and was for a long time the only version known to the Persian Church. It was translated into Persian and various manuscripts of this translation have survived.

The first printed version of the ancient Syriac version Peshitta New Testament was produced in Vienna in 1555. The editor was J. A. Widmanstaat and the printer was Michael Zimmermann, who used types prepared by that interesting French orientalist, Guillaume Postel.

Many other editions of the ancient Syriac text of the Bible (both Old and New Testaments) were printed and many manuscript editions were made by the Nestorian Church in Persia. But it was not until the coming of the American Board missionaries that in 1846 a diglot edition of the whole Bible was printed at the mission press in Urmiah. This was done under the supervision of Edward Breath, the missionary printer who himself designed and cut the type, basing his design on the solid simple script of the manuscripts of the local churches.

Perkins, Wright and other early missionaries were most assiduous in their preparation of editions of the Old and New Testaments, but their editions were in the dialect of the Nestorians of Urmiah and so were not understood by the mountain Nestorians of Kurdistan. Thus in 1881 Benjamin Larabee with a committee of Nestorian scholars began a revision of the earlier version in order to make it more widely acceptable. This they succeeded in doing: the work was sent to press in 1887 and in 1893 it was published by the American Bible Society in New York. The value of the early American missionaries' work in the establishment of modern literary Syriac has already been mentioned; the publication of the 1893 Bible set a seal on this valuable labour.

The contribution of the Jewish community to the preservation and dissemination of the Old Testament was very important but cannot be more than mentioned here.

Confining ourselves to the Bible in Persian, we find it surprising that the long Roman Catholic missionary endeavours in Persia did not result in the publication of any portion of the Bible in Persian. No doubt various missionaries in Persia at various times translated various portions for their own use, and we have the curious *Dastane Massih* and the *Dastane San Pedro* of Jerome Xavier, the former being a harmony of the Gospels interspersed with many stories from the Apocryphal Gospels and the latter a life of St Peter with a strong Roman emphasis. The first effort to translate the whole Bible into Persian was, as we have seen, made by Nader Shah in 1741.

Meanwhile in Europe, oriental scholars were at work: an ardent Protestant, Ludovic de Dieu, in his *Rudimenta Linguae Persicae* (1639) printed a translation of the first two chapters of Genesis. These were based on Jacob Ta'usi's version of the Pentateuch which first appeared in Constantinople in 1546 and was later used for Walton's Polyglott Bible (1654–7) – which also used early manuscripts of the Gospels in the possession of Edward Pococke, first professor of Arabic at Oxford.

In 1657 Abraham Whelock's translation of the Gospels into Persian was published in London. It was naturally consulted by later translators, including Martyn, but was found to contain too many Arabic expressions to be of much use.

It was left to the Protestant missionary movement of the nineteenth century to achieve the publication of an adequate translation of the whole Bible. The first move in this direction came from India and that remarkable man, Claudius Buchanan, who correctly forecast that: 'It will form an epoch in the history of Persia when a version of the Old and New Testament shall begin to be known generally in that country.' (Buchanan, *Christian Researches in Asia*, p. 99.)

The start was made at Fort William College, Calcutta, of which Buchanan was vice-principal. A translation of the Gospels was begun under the supervision of Colonel R. H. Colebrook, with two native assistants, Mirza Sabat (an Arab) and Mirza Fitrat (an Indian). The Gospels of Luke and Matthew were translated, and in 1805 800 copies of each were printed and deposited for sale in the

Bibliotheca Biblica at Calcutta (see the BFBS report for 1810). Martyn's arrival on the scene in 1808 gave great impetus to the work, but he soon found his collaborators unreliable and unsatisfactory since neither had Persian as his mother tongue. He therefore decided to go to Persia to complete the translation of the New Testament with the help of Persians in Persia. His trials and death in Turkey have already been described.

The publication of his version in St Peterburg in 1815 seems to have been due to a chance meeting between Sir Gore Ouseley, the British Minister, and Prince Galitzin, the head of the recently-formed Russian Bible Society. The work took a year to print and Ouseley corrected the proofs. But in spite of all the care taken, this first edition was so full of errors and omissions that it was not of much use and soon had to be replaced by revised editions.

Martyn's translation was to become the basis for all future work on producing a satisfactory text, and marks the beginning of the modern Persian Bible. As we have seen, however, his version was by no means the first. An earlier attempt which deserves mention was that made by Father Leopoldo Sebastiani, who as a member of the Roman Catholic mission had spent many years in Persia. His translation of the Gospels was published in 1813 (in an edition of 1,000 copies) by the Protestant Calcutta Bible Society and a revised edition of St Matthew's Gospel was published by the Baptist Mission Press of Serampore in 1816.

The second edition of Martyn's version was printed in London in 1816 and the third in 1827. From then on, for the next fifty years, it held the field as the standard translation of the New Testament.

But by the time Bruce came to Persia in 1869 it was generally felt that a substantial revision was needed and also that a new version of the Old Testament should be undertaken. A previous version of the Old Testament had been made by William Glen of the Scottish Missionary Society in Astrakhan. In 1830 Glen had been asked to translate the poetical and prophetic books of the Bible. When the work was completed it was felt that only the Psalms and the Book of Proverbs were satisfactory enough to print and they were published in 1835 and 1841 respectively by the BFBS. Eventually the whole of Glen's translation of the Bible was published by 'The Committee of Foreign Missions Connected with the United Associate Synod of Scotland' at Edinburgh in 1846. This, as far as I know, was the first translation of the whole Bible into Persian to be published. Meanwhile, as we have seen (p. 149), Bruce's work on the revision of the New Testament and a new translation of the Old, occupied much of his time.

From the earliest years of his stay in Persia, Bruce was in touch with the BFBS which paid the salary of his *munshee* or secretary. In 1878 the Society's representative, Mr Watt, spent Christmas with the Bruces and chose Benjamin Badal as a colporteur. Badal's career, which lasted forty-one years, was one of heroic devotion to the spread of the Gospel in every part of Iran. Badal was one outstanding example of a class of men – mainly Armenians – who in the face of constant persecution and opposition travelled all over the country selling and distributing Bibles and Gospels, thus helping to realise Buchanan's prediction about the spread of the Bible in Persia. His daughter, Mrs Margaret Nakhosteen, wife of the first Persian Bible Society representative, remembers her father's cheerfulness while he was at home in spite of the constant danger of imprisonment, bastinado-beating or stoning which faced him every time he went on a journey.

In 1880 CMS and the Bible Society agreed that Bruce should be the Bible Society's representative in Iran, and Persia took its place in the list of BFBS foreign agencies. In 1881 Bruce landed in England with his completed version of the Persian New Testament and the text was passed to Professor E. H. Palmer who revised it before it was published in an edition of 6,000 copies. For this work Bruce was made a D.D. of Trinity College Dublin, *Honoris causa*. Bruce continued to serve as BFBS representative until 1888. In 1890 a replacement in the person of James A. Douglas came but he soon returned to England. In 1891 Mr Hodgson of the CMS in Baghdad took over and the following year made Bushire his headquarters. He organised an efficient band of colporteurs with Aga Mackertich in Julfa and Yakub Galustian in Baghdad and sub-depots in Sultanabad and Kermanshah.

In 1895 the new Bible house was dedicated in Julfa and this year also saw the publication of Bruce's complete revision of the Persian Bible which was printed for the BFBS in Leipzig. For this pioneer work, which had taken him over twenty years, Bruce was made an honorary D.D. of Oxford.

Hodgson went on to Turkey in 1895 and Bishop Stuart took his place as a temporary measure until C. E. G. Tisdall, brother of the CMS missionary already in Persia, relieved him in 1898. In 1902 the importation of the Scriptures was forbidden and this ban continued until 1906, though very small numbers were allowed in from time to time.

In 1908 Tisdall was transferred to Singapore and his place taken by Theodore Irrisch, a remarkable linguist and scholar who unfortunately died in 1911. In 1913 Alexander Hope was appointed agent and served until 1936. During his period of service a new Bible house was opened in Tehran (1914) which henceforth became the centre of the work. On Hope's retirement, the position of representative of the BFBS was taken by Adl Nakhosteen, who served until 1966 and did much to consolidate the work – supervising the erection of the fine new Bible house adjacent to the American Mission compound.

There is no doubt that Bible colportage was 'the simplest and least questionable method of evangelising' – to quote the Society's historian. Many hundreds of thousands of Bibles, Testaments and portions have been distributed over the years: for instance, during the period 1804–1904, 17,412 portions in Judaeo-Persian, 20,000 whole Bibles, 64,000 New Testaments and New Testament and Psalms, and 179,481 Gospels and other portions of the Bible – and this during a period when the reading population was never more than 100,000.

Today the work goes on under the control of Aga Tatavoos Michaelian, and a new generation of colporteurs continue the work of Benjamin Badal and his colleagues, though with very few of the difficulties which they experienced.

BIBLIOGRAPHY

The Bibliography which follows consists merely of those works which I have consulted during the writing of this book. I have in preparation a fuller bibliography of Christianity in Iran, which it is hoped will be published in due course by the Armaghan Institute in Tehran.

The manuscript archives of the various missionary societies also contain a mass of relevant material, which I have been not able to consider and which still awaits the investigation of scholars.

Unless otherwise stated, all books are published in London.

GENERAL WORKS

Avery, P., *Modern Iran*, 2nd rev. edn. (1967).
Banani, Amin, *The Modernisation of Iran* (Stanford, Calif., 1961).
Boulnois, L., *The Silk Road* (1966).
Cuming, G. J. (ed.), *Studies in Church History*, vol. 6 (Cambridge, 1967). Note especially the article by Bishop Stephen Neill, 'The History of Mission as an Academic Discipline'.
Descombaz, S., *Histoire des Missions Evangéliques* (Paris, 1860).
Donaldson, Dwight M., *The Shi'ite Religion: A History of Islam in Persia and Irak* (1933).
Flaschmeier, H. R., *Geschichte der Evangelischen Weltmission* (Giessen, 1963).
Levy, R., *The Social Structure of Islam* (Cambridge, 1957).
Marshall, T. W. M., *Christian Missions: Their Agents, Their Methods and Their Results* (London and Brussels, 1852). 3 volumes (almost comically anti-Protestant).
Newcomb, Harvey, *A Cyclopedia of Missions* (New York, 1855).
Richter, Julius, *A History of Protestant Missions in the Near East* (1910).
Saunders, J. J., *A History of Mediaeval Islam* (1965).
Wardlaw Thompson, R. and Johnson, A. N., *British Foreign Missions* (1899).
Warneck, G., *History of Protestant Missions* (1901).
Wilson, A. T., *A Bibliography of Persia* (Oxford, 1930)
—*Persia* (1932).

PART ONE

Atiya, Aziz S., *A History of Eastern Christianity* (1968). Illus. (of very limited use).
Brown, L. W., *The Indian Christians of St Thomas* (Cambridge, 1956).
Browne, L. E., *The Eclipse of Christianity in Asia* (Cambridge, 1933).
Burkitt, F. C., *Early Eastern Christianity* (1904).
Chabot, J. B. (ed.), *Synodicon Orientale ou Recueil de Synodes Nestoriens* (Paris, 1902).

BIBLIOGRAPHY

'Chronica Ecclesiae Arbelensis et Idiomate Syriaco in Latinum Vertit Franciscus Zorell S.J.' (Rome, 1927), *Orientalia Christiana*, vol. VIII, 4.
'Chronique de Seert. Histoire Nestorienne inédite (Chronique de Seert) par Mgr Addai Scher' (Paris, 1907, 1909), in *Patrologia Orientalis*, ed. Graffin and Nau, vol. IV., part 3.
Cosmas Indicopleustes, *The Christian Topography*, translated from the Greek and edited by J. W. McCrindle (Hakluyt Society, 1897).
Dawson, C., *The Mongol Mission* (1955).
Delacrois, S., (ed.), *Histoire Universelle des Missions Catholiques* (Paris 1956–8). 4 volumes; especially vol. 1, chapter 6, by J. Richard, 'Les Missions chez les Mongols aux 13e et 14e Siècles', and vol. 2, Chapter 5, by Bernard de Vaulx, 'Éveil Missionaire de la France au Levant, en Perse . . . 1608–74'.
Doble, G. H., 'St Ivo: Bishop and Confessor Patron of the Town of St Ives' (1934), in *Laudate,* vol. 12, pp. 149–56.
Foster, J., *The Church of the T'ang Dynasty* (1939).
Gordon, A. E., *Asian Cristology [sic] and the Mahayana, A Reprint of the century-old Indian Church History by Thomas Yeates and Further Investigation of the Religion of the Orient* (Tokyo, 1921). Gordon's facts are interesting but his deductions are dubious. Yeates' book was first published in 1818.
Hallberg, I., 'L'extrême-Orient dans la Littérature et la Cartographie, de l'Occident des XIIIe, XIVe et XVe Siècles'. (Goteborg, 1904), in *Goteborgs Kungl Vetenskapsoch Vitterhets.* Samhalles handlingar, vol. v., pp. 371–5.
Holm, F., *The Nestorian Monument* 1909).
— *My Nestorian Adventures in China* (1924).
Labourt, J., *Le Christianisme dans l'Empire Perse sous la Dynastie Sassanide (224–632)* (Paris, 1904).
— *De Timotheo I, Nest. Patr. et Christianorum Orientalium Condicione sub Chaliphis* (Paris, 1904).
Legge, F., *Forerunners and Rivals of Christianity* (Cambridge, 1915). 2 volumes.
Mingana, A., 'The Early Spread of Christianity in Central Asia' (1925), in *Bulletin John Rylands Library*, Manchester, vol. 9, no. 2, pp. 297–371.
— 'Early Spread of Christianity in India' (1926), in *Bulletin John Rylands Library*, Manchester, vol. 10, pp. 435–514.
Nau, F., *L'Expansion Nestorienne en Asie* (Paris, 1914).
O'Leary, de Lacy, *The Syriac Church and Fathers: A Brief Review of the Subject* (1909). The title exactly describes it.
Pelliot, P., *Mongols et Papes aux XIIIe et XIVe Siècles* (Paris, 1922).
— 'L'Évêché Nestorien de Khumdan et Sarag' (1928), in *T'Oung Pao*, vol. 25, pp. 91ff.
Sachau, C. E., *Zur Ausbreitung des Christentums in Asien* (Berlin, 1919). *Abh. der preuss Akademie der Wissenschaft Jhrg. 1919 P.h klasse no. 1.*
Saeki, P. Y., *The Nestorian Monument in China* (1916).
Streit, R., *Bibliotheca Missionum: Tome IV, Asiatische Missions Literatur 1245–1599* (Aix-La-Chapelle, 1928).
Takakusu, J., 'The Name of 'Messiah' Found in a Buddhist Book, the

Nestorian Missionary Adam Presbyter, Papas of China, translating a Buddhist Sutra' (1896), in: T'Oung Pao, vol. 7, pp. 589ff.

Tisserant, Eugène, 'Église Nestorienne' in *Dictionnaire de Théologie Catholique*, vol. 2, pp. 158ff. The best account of the history of the Nestorian Church.

Vine, A. R., *The Nestorian Churches* (1937). A reasonably complete sketch to the present century.

Vööbus, A., 'Celibacy: A Requirement for Admission to Baptism in the Early Syrian Church' (Stockholm, 1951), in *Papers of the Estonian Theological Society in Exile*, no. 1.

Wigram, W. A., *An Introduction to the History of the Assyrian Church . . . 100–640 A.D.* (1910). Still a standard work.

Wright, W., *A Short History of Syriac Literature* (1894).

Zachariah of Mitylene, *The Syriac Chronicle Known as that of Zachariah of Mitylene*, translated by F. J. Hamilton and E. W. Brooks (London, 1889), pp. 329–31. It describes a missionary journey from Persia to evangelise the Huns.

Zaehner, R., *The Dawn and Twilight of Zoroastrianism* (1961).

PART TWO

Antelmi, Léonce, *La Vie de Messire François Picquet, Consul de France et de Hollande à Alep, Ensuite Évêque de Césaropole puis de Babylone, Vicaire Apostolique en Perse avec Titre d'Ambassadeur du Roy auprès du Roy de Perse . . .* (Paris, 1732).

Arvieux, Laurent d', *Mémoires du Chevalier d'Arvieux, Envoyé Extraordinaire du Roy à la Porte, Consul d'Alep, d'Alger, de Tripoli et autres Echelles du Levant . . .* par le R. P. Jean Baptiste Labat (Paris, 1735). 6 volumes: vol. 6., pp 81–158, contains an account of François Picquet and reprints a number of his letters from Persia.

[Chick, H.], *A Chronicle of the Carmelites in Persia and the Papal Mission of the Seventeenth and Eighteenth Centuries* (1939), 2 volumes, large 4to., illus. Immensely valuable, if its Catholic bias is allowed for.

Chinon, Gabriel de, *Relations Nouvelles du Levant* (Lyon, 1671).

Gollancz, Sir H. (ed.), *Chronicle of Events 1623–1733 Relating to the Settlement of the Carmelites in Mesopotamia* (Oxford, 1927).

Goormachtig, Bernard O. P., *Histoire de la Mission Dominicaine en Mésopotamie et en Kurdistan* (Rome, 1896–8).

Gouvea, A., *Histoire Orientale, des grands progrès de l'Eglise Cathol. Apost. et Rom . . . Composée en Langue Portugaise . . . et Tournée en Français par F. Jean-Baptiste de Glen* (Anvers, 1609).

Goyau, G., *Un Précurseur, François Picquet, Consul de Louis XIV en Alep et Évêque de Babylone* (Paris, 1942).

Ignace, Fr Berthold de Ste Anne, *Histoire de la Mission de la Perse* (Brussels and Paris, 1888).

Jesuit Fathers, *Lettres Édifiantes et Curieuses concernant l'Asie, l'Afrique et l'Amérique . . . Publiées sous la Direction de M. L. Aimé-Martin* (Paris,

1838). Vol. 1 contains matters on Persia. There are many other earlier editions.

Juan de Persia, *Relaciones* (Valladolid, 1604).

[Leemens, L.], Hierarchia Latina Orientis, Medianto S. Congregatione de Propaganda Fide Instituta (1622–1922) (part II) (1923), in *Orientalia Christiana*, vol. II, no. 1, pp. 265–313. Covers the Diocese of Isfahan.

Loennertz, R., *La Société des Frères Pérégrinants: Études sur l'Orient Dominicain* (Rome, 1937).

Maclagen, E., *The Jesuits and the Great Mogul* (1932).

Minorsky, V., *The Middle East in Western Politics* (1940). Reprinted from the *Journal Royal Central Asian Society*, vol 27, pp. 427–61. Deals with the thirteenth, fifteenth and seventeenth centuries.

— *La Perse au XVe Siècle entre la Turquie et la Venise* (Paris, 1933).

Phillippus a Sancta Trinité, *Voyage d'Orient du R. P. Phillipe de la Saincte Trinité Carme Deschaussé* (Lyon, 1652).

Rabbath, Antoine S. J. (ed.), *Documents inédits pour Servir à l'Histoire du Christianisme en Orient* (Paris, 1907–10). 2 volumes, all published. All from Catholic sources.

Tamarati, M., *L'Église Géorgienne des Origines jusqu'à Nos Jours* (Rome, 1910).

Terzorio, P. Clement, da, *Le Missioni dei Minori Cappucini sunto Storico*: Vol. 6, *Turchia Asiatica* (Rome, 1920).

Wilson, A. T. (trans.), 'History of the Mission of the Fathers of the Society of Jesus, Established in Persia by the Rev. Alexander of Rhodes' (1923–5), in *BSOAS*, vol. 3, pp. 675–706. The original, printed in 1659, was by Father Jacques de Machault.

PART THREE

Ainsworth, W. F., *Researches in Assyria, Babylonia and Chaldea forming part of the Labours of the Euphrates Expedition* (1838). Note especially p. 343 map, frontispiece and folding geological charts.

— *A Personal Narrative of the Euphrates Expedition . . .* (1888). 2 volumes.

Anderson, Rufus, *History of the Missions of the American Board of Commissioners for Foreign Missions to the Oriental Churches* (Boston, 1873). 2 volumes.

Archbishop's Assyrian Mission, *Quarterly Papers*, nos 1–99 (1890–1915). Full of interesting material on the history, folklore and condition of the Nestorians. The British Museum has an almost complete set.

Avril, Adolphe d', *La Chaldée Chrétienne* (Paris, 1892).

Badger, G. P., *The Nestorians and Their Rituals, with the Narrative of a Mission to Mesopotamia and Coordistan in 1842–1844 and of a Late Visit to Those Countries in 1850* (1852). 2 volumes.

Bassett, James, *Persia: Eastern Mission: A Narrative of the Founding and Fortunes of the Eastern Persia Mission* (Philadelphia, 1890).

Bishop, Mrs (née Isabella L. Bird), *Journeys in Persia and Kurdistan including a Summer in the Upper Karun Region and a Visit to the Nestorian Rayahs* (1891).

Bolshakoff, Serge, *The Foreign Missions of the Russian Orthodox Church* (1943).

Boré, Eugene, *Correspondance et Mémoires d'un Voyageur en Orient* (Paris, 1840). 2 volumes.

Brittlebank, W., *Persia During the Famine* (1873).

Bruce, Robert, 'Persia in its Relation to the Kingdom of God'. Part One: The Medo-Persian Empire and Israel; Part Two: The Early Christian Church in Persia; Part Three: Muhammedanism in Persia; Part Four: The Church Missionary Society's Persia Mission 1881–1882. All in *C.M. Intelligencer*, vol. 6 N.S., pp. 654–64, 734–41; and Vol. N.S., pp. 24–31 and pp. 104–14.

Brühl, J. H., *The Ten Tribes: Who are they?* (London, Operative Jewish Converts Institution, 1880). Brühl believed that Persian Jews are the lost ten tribes of Israel.

Buchanan, Claudius, *Christian Researches in Asia, with Notices of the translation of the Scriptures into Oriental Languages* (1840).

Cameron, K. W., *Manuscripts of Horatio Southgate* (1937). Reprinted from *The American Church Monthly*, vol. 42, no. 4 (October, 1937), pp 155–73.

Canton, W., *History of the British and Foreign Bible Society* (1904–1910). 5 volumes, up to 1904 only. For later history, see Roe.

Cash, W. Wilson, *Report on the Persia Mission: A Record of a Visit to the Persia Mission by the Rev. W. Wilson Cash, General Secretary, during April and May 1928* (1928).

A Century of Mission Work in Iran (Persia) 1834–1934 (Beirut, American Press, 1935).

Coan, F. G., *Yesterdays in Persia and Kurdistan* (Claremont, Calif., 1939).

Cutts, E. L., *Christians under the Crescent in Asia* (1877).

Dehqani-Taft, H. B., *Design of My World* (World Christian Books, 1959).

Dugat, G., *Histoire des Orientalistes* (Paris, n.d.). Includes a note on Kazem-Beg.

Elder, John, *History of the American Presbyterian Mission to Iran* (Tehran, c. 1962).

Fischel, W. J., 'The Bible in Persian Translation: A Contribution to the History of Bible Translations in Persia and India' (1952), in *Harvard Theological Review*, pp. 4–45. A very valuable survey with very full bibliographical references.

— 'The Jews of Persia under the Kajar Dynasty' (1950), in *Jewish Social Studies*, vol. 12, pp. 119–60.

Fiske, D. T., *Fidelia Fiske* (edited by William Guest, 1870). A shortened version of the American biography.

French, T. V., 'The Bishop of Lahore's Journal in Persia' (1883–4), in *C.M. Intelligencer*, vol. 8 N.S., pp. 660–9 and vol. 9 N.S., pp. 91–7.

Gaster, Gwen, *Our Blind Family* (1959).

Gidney, W. T., *Sites and Scenes: A Description of Missions to Jews in Eastern Lands* (1897–8). 2 volumes: vol. 1, pp. 73–101 (Persia).

— *History of the London Society for Promoting Christianity amongst the Jews 1809–1908* (1908).

Grant, Asahel, *The Nestorians: or the Lost Tribes, Containing Evidence of Their Identity* (1841).

Halsted, T. D., *Our Missions: Being a History of the Principal Missionary Transactions of the London Society for Promoting Christianity among the Jews* (1866).

Heravi, M., *Iranian-American Diplomacy* (Brooklyn, N.Y., 1969).

Holmes, John, *Historical Sketches of the Missions of the United Brethren*, 2nd edn. (1827).

Hoole, E., *The Year-Book of Missions* (1847).

Joseph, John, *The Nestorians and Their Muslim Neighbours: A Study of Western Influence on their Relations* (Princeton, N.J., 1961). An excellent work to which I am greatly indebted.

Kratschkowski, I. J., *Die Russische Arabistik: Umrisse ihrer Entwicklung* (Leipzig, 1957). For later career of Alexander Kazem-Beg.

Laurie, T., *Dr Grant and the Mountain Nestorians* (Boston, 1853).

Lyko, Dieter, *Gründung Wachstum und Leben der Evangelischen Christlichen Kirchen in Iran* (Leiden, 1964). Contains a good deal of useful raw material uncritically collected.

McNeill, — *Memoir of the Rt Hon Sir John McNeil, GCB, and of his Second Wife, Elizabeth Wilson*, by their grand-daughter (1910).

Malcolm, Napier, *Five Years in a Persian Town* (1905).

Malech, George David, *History of the Syrian Nation and the Old Evangelical Apostolic Church of the East* (Minneapolis, 1910), edited by his son, George Nestorius Malech, Archdeacon.

Martyn, Henry, *Journals and Letters*, edited by S. Wilberforce (1837). 2 volumes.

Miller, W. McE., *Ten Muslims Meet Christ* (Grand Rapids, Michigan, 1969). Biographies of ten Persian Christians.

Mission Problems in New Persia. A Report of the All-Persia Intermission Conference of 1926. For Private Circulation (American Press, Beirut, 1926).

Missionary Register . . . Containing an Abstract of the Proceedings of the Principal Missionary and Bible Societies throughout the World (1813–56). Volumes 1–43 all published. A mine of information.

Montefiore, Sir Moses and Lady, *Diaries* (1890). 2 volumes.

Owen, John, *The History of the Origin and First Ten Years of the British and Foreign Bible Society* (London, 1816). 3 volumes. Vol. 1, pp. 265–6, a footnote contains the full text of Fath-Ali Shah's letter to Sir Gore Ouseley thanking him for Martyn's translation of the New Testament.

Padwick, Constance E., *Henry Martyn, Confessor of the Faith* (1923).

Perkins, Justin, *Residence of Eight Years in Persia among the Nestorian Christians* (Andover, Mass., 1843).

Persia Mission Letter, no. 1 (1920)–6 (1923), continued as: *Persia Diocesan Letter*, no. 7 (1923)–no. 29 (1934), continued as: *Iran Diocesan Letter*, no. 30–100 (1968). The only complete file I know of is in the possession of the Iran Diocesan Association in London.

Piolet, J. B. (ed.), *Les Missions Catholiques Françaises au XIX⁰ Siècle* (Paris, c. 1900).

Richards, J. R., *The Open Road in Persia* (CMS, 1933).

Roe, J. M., *A History of the British and Foreign Bible Society 1905–1954* (London, BFBS, 1965). For the earlier history, see Canton, W. and Owen, J.

Southgate, Horatio, *Narrative of a Tour through Armenia, Kurdistan, Persia and Mesopotamia* (New York, 1840). 2 volumes.

Sparroy, Wilfred, *Persian Children of the Royal Family. The Narrative of an English Tutor at the Court of H.I.H. Zillu's-Sultan GCSI* (1902).

Speer, R. E., *'The Hakim Sahib'. The Foreign Doctor: A Biography of Joseph Plumb Cochrane M.D. of Persia* (1911).

Stern, H. A., *Dawnings of Light in the East with Biblical, Historical and Statistical Notices of Persons and Places Visited during a Mission to the Jews in Persia, Coordistan and Mesopotamia* (1854).

Stileman, C. H., 'The Subjects of the Shah' (*CMS*, 1902), pp. vi, 96. Many illustrations.

— 'The Outlook in Persia' (1907), in *C.M. Review*, vol. 58, pp. 75–9.

[Tisdall, W. St Clair], 'Christianity in the Persian Empire—Present and Past' (1896), in *C.M. Intelligencer*, vol. 21 N.S., pp. 401–16.

Wheeler, W. R. (ed.), *The Crisis Decade* (N.Y., 1950), pp. 155–61. Chapter 12: 'Closed and Open Doors in Iran', by Cady H. Allen.

Wigram, W. A., *Britain's Smallest Ally. A Brief Account of the Assyrian Nation in the Great War* (1920).

— *The Assyrian Settlement*. Foreword by the Archbishop of Canterbury (1922).

— *The Assyrians and Their Neighbours* (1929).

Wishard, John G., *Twenty Years in Persia* (1908).

Wolff, Joseph, *Sketch of the Life and Journal of the Rev. J. Wolff, Missionary to Palestine and Persia* (Norwich, 1827).

— *Researches and Missionary Labours among the Jews, Mohammedans and Other Sects during his Travels between the Years 1831 and 1834*. Published by the author (London 1835) and printed at the Church Missionary Society's Press in Malta.

Woodroffe, Janet, 'Persian Girls and Christian Education' (1927), *CM Review*, vol. 78, pp. 342–51.

Yonan, Isaac Malek, *The Beloved Physician of Tehran* (Cokesbury Press, Nashville, 1934). A life of Dr Saeed Khan Kurdistani.

Zwemer, S. M., 'Persia Faces the Future' (1927), in *CM Review*, vol. 78, pp. 42–50.

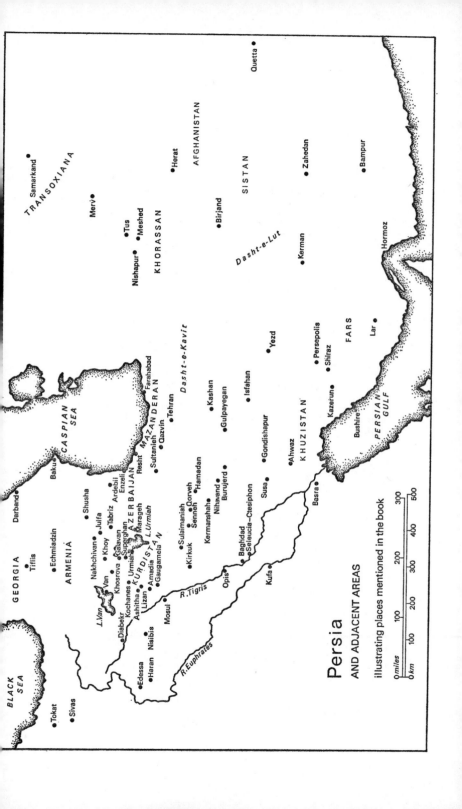

Persia
AND ADJACENT AREAS
illustrating places mentioned in the book

Index

Abbas I (Shah), 60–9, 151
Abbasid caliphate, 35–6, 38
Abqar, Kings of Edessa, 17
Afghan Invasion of Persia, 74–5
Aidin (Miss Nouhie), 167, 169, 174
A'ina-i Haqq Nama, 62
Antioch, 18, 21, 23, 25, 42
American Board of Commissioners for
  Foreign Missions, 102ff., 110–111
Alborz College (Tehran), 134, 143
Alexander (Dr E. W.), 136, 137–8
Alopen, 43, 45
Archbishop of Canterbury's Mission,
  124–132
Arghun Khan, 50–1
Armenia, 52, 53, 63–4, 70
Armenian Church, theology of, 23–4
Armenians, 26, 48, 66, 68, 69, 71,
  72, 75, 76, 79, 91, 110, 133, 149–
  50
— forcibly removed to Persia, 63–4
Assassins, 38, 47, 50
Astrakhan, 77, 100, 148
Augustinian Hermits, 59, 62, 68–9,
  73, 77

Babis, *see* Bahais
Babowai (Catholicos), 27
Badal (Benjamin), 180
Badger (Rev. G. P.), 107-8, 124–5
Baghdad, 35, 49, 101, 113, 114,
  151
Bahais, 113, 114, 118, 158–9, 163
Bakhtiaris, 119, 157–8, 161
Bar Sauma (Bp of Nisibis), 26–7
Basel Missionary Society, 100
Baskerville (Howard), 140–1
Bassett (Rev. James), 116, 133–5, 136
Beit d'Edrai (Synod of), 27
Bernard de Sainte Thérèse (Père),
  65, 69, 70, 72
Bible Churchmen's Missionary
  Society (BCMS), 175–6
Bible, Judaeo-Persian, 60, 122
Bible: translation into Persian, 89–
  93, 99, 134, 136, 147, 149, 177–81
Bird (Mary), 155–6, 157, 162
Bishop (Mrs Isabella), description of
  mission in Julfa, 152–3, 154
Boré (Eugène), 79–81
Breath (Edward), 104–5, 177

British and Foreign Bible Society
  (BFBS), 98, 138, 147–8, 170, 178,
  179–81
Browne (Rev. W. H.), 126–8, 130–2
Bruce (Dr Robert), 115, 116, 118,
  134, 148–52, 153, 162, 179, 180
Buchanan (Claudius), 88, 89, 178
Buddhists, 28, 42, 44, 50
Bushire, 113, 118, 162

Capuchin Friars Minor, 69–70, 72,
  77
Carmelites, 65ff.
Carr (Dr Donald), 119, 121, 156–8,
  159, 162, 165, 166
Central Asia. Expansion of
  Christianity in, 39–40
Ceylon, 40–1
Chalcedon (Council of), 25–6
Chaldean Church (Uniate), 78–9
Chezaud (Aimé, S. J.), 71, 77–8
China, Nestorian expansion in, 42–5
Christological controversy, 23–5
Christoffel Blindenmission, 171–2
Church's Ministry among the Jews
  (CMJ), 96–7, 112–23
Church Missionary Society (CMS), 90,
  100, 101, 115, 124, 134, 147–75
Cluzel (Mons.), 80–2, 110
Constitutional Movement, 120–1,
  140–1, 156, 160–1
Covenant of the Prophet, 33

Dastane Massih, 62, 178
Dehqani–Tafti (Bp Hassan), 173,
  174–5
Dominicans, 52, 74, 77, 84, 102
Don Juan of Persia, 61
Du Mans (P. Raphael), 63, 72
Dutch East India Co., 64–5, 89

East India Co., 67–8, 89
Edessa, 16–17, 20–1, 26, 34, 41
Edinburgh (later, Scottish) Mission-
  ary Society, 98–100, 179
Elder (Dr John), 168
Ephesus (First Council of), 24–5
Esselstyn (Rev. L. F.), 138–9

Fath-Ali Shah, 93
Fiske (Fidelia), 109

190

Fort William College, 89–91, 178
Franciscans, 52, 73
Fratres Unitores, 53
French (The), in Persia, 69ff.
French (T. V. Bp of Lahore), 100, 148, 150–1, 156

Garland (Archdeacon, J. R.), 119–22
Georgia, 52, 53, 70, 87
Georgians, 49
— forcibly removed to Persia, 66–7
Ghazan Khan, 47, 52
Glen (Dr Wm.), 99–100, 179–80
Gondishapur, 18
Grant (Dr Asahel), 104–7
Gregory XIII (Pope), 59, 60
Gulpayegan, 116, 119, 121

Haas (F.), 100, 102, 148–9
Hakim, (Mirza Jolinoos), 119, 122
Hamadan, 29, 70, 75, 76, 110, 113–14, 116–17, 136–7, 139, 144
Hawkes (Rev. J. W.), 136
Hoecker (C. F. W.), 88–9
Holmes (Dr G. W.), 136, 137
Hormoz Island, 59, 62, 68
Hulagu, 49, 50
Hussein (Shia martyr), 35, 38

Il Khans, 48ff.
India: Nestorian expansion in, 40–1
Indo-European Telegraph Co., 136, 148, 159, 165
Innocent IV (Pope), 48
International Mission, 140, 176
Isaac (Bp), 20–1
Isfahan, 29, 61, 65ff., 79, 83, 89, 96, 99, 115, 117, 120, 122, 159–61, 162, 171
Ives (St), 46

Jesuits, 62, 71, 77
Jews, 33, 72, 75, 96–98, 112–123, 133, 158, 170
— legal disabilities of, 115, 117–8
— persecuted under the Sassanians, 26, 28
Jordan (Dr), 134
Julfa (Isfahan), 63, 64, 67, 69, 73, 74–5, 77, 118, 120, 134, 148–9, 156, 165

Kashan, 96, 114, 116, 118
Kavad (King), 27–8, 39
Kazem-Beg (Alexander), 99–100
Kazerun, 96, 115, 118
Kerman, 116, 122, 154, 157, 159, 160, 162, 167, 168, 169, 171, 174

Kermanshah, 113, 114, 139–40
Khorassan, 22, 29, 35, 97
Khosro Anushiravan (King), 28–9
Kirkuk, Martyrs of, 25–6
Kochanes (Qudshanis), 78, 127–8, 130–1
Kurds, 106–8, 124–5, 127, 130–1, 141, 176

Lazarist Fathers, 74, 80–3
Linton (Bp J. H.), 122, 161, 162, 163, 164–6, 170, 175
Little Brothers and Sisters of Jesus, 83–4
Lutheran Orient Mission, 176

Maclean (Canon A. J.), 126–7, 129, 131–2
Magi, 16, 21, 28
Malcolm (Sir John), 87, 91, 92
Malcolm (Rev. Napier), 157, 159, 160, 175
Manichaeism, 15, 28, 42
Mar Aba (Catholicos), 28–9, 39
Mar Shimun XIV, 106–8, 124–5
Marageh, 49, 51, 52–3
Marco Polo, 40
Markabta (Synod of), 22–3
Marouta (Bp of Maypherqat), 20–1
Martyn (Henry), 89–95, 99, 147, 178–9
Mazdakites, 13, 15, 27–8
Merv, 29, 39, 40, 49
Meshed, 83, 112, 138–9
Miller (W. M.), 145
Mizan al Haqq, 100
Monastic Life in Nestorian church, 30–2
Mongols, 38–9, 48ff.
Mongol Embassies to Europe, 48, 50ff.
Montefiore (Sir Moses), 114–5, 148
Moravian missionaries, 88–9

Nader Shah, 75–6, 112
Nasr-ud-din Shah, 82, 115, 156
Nestorius (Bp of Constantinople), 23–5
Nicaea (Council of), 20–1, 23
Nicholas IV (Pope), 51
Nur Ayin Blind Institute, 172
Nurullah (Mirza) *jnr.*, 117–19, 121, 122, 134

Pahlavi inscriptions in India, 41
— — — China, 45
Papa (Bishop), 18–19
Parthians, 13–14, 16–17, 63

192